FREEDOMBIRD DESIGN

Cactus Coloring Book

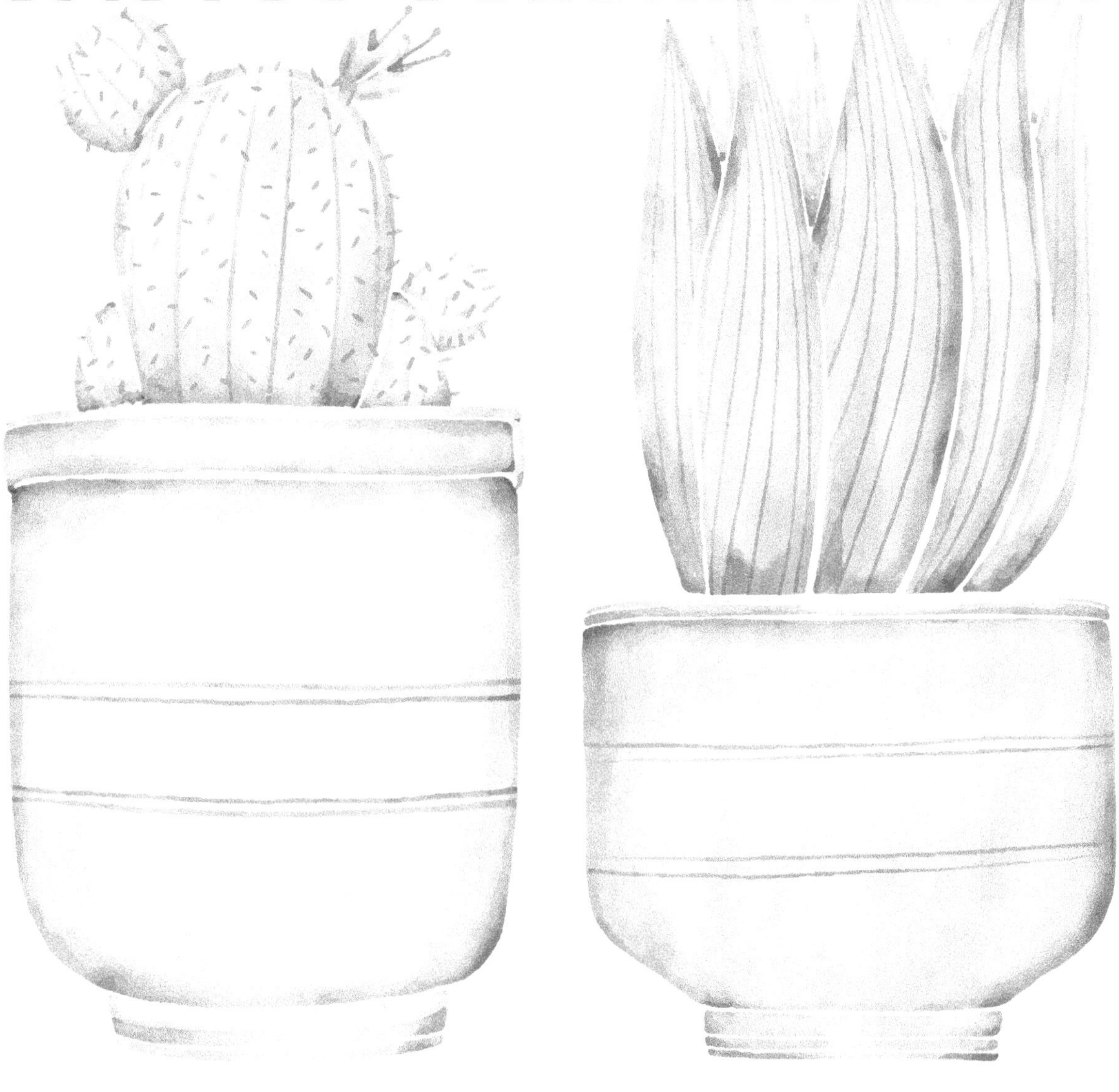

ISBN-13: 978-1975984144

ISBN-10: 1975984145

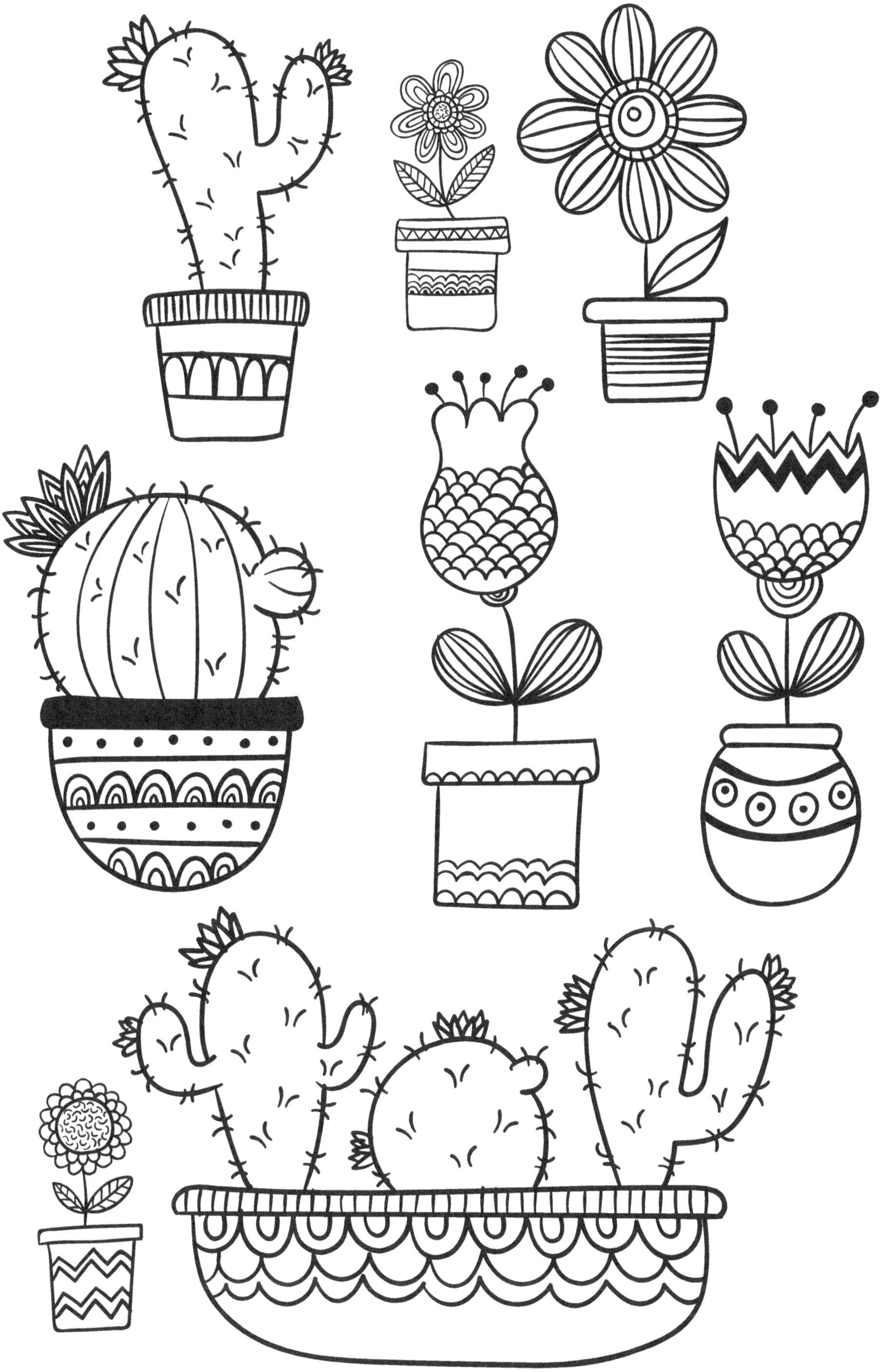

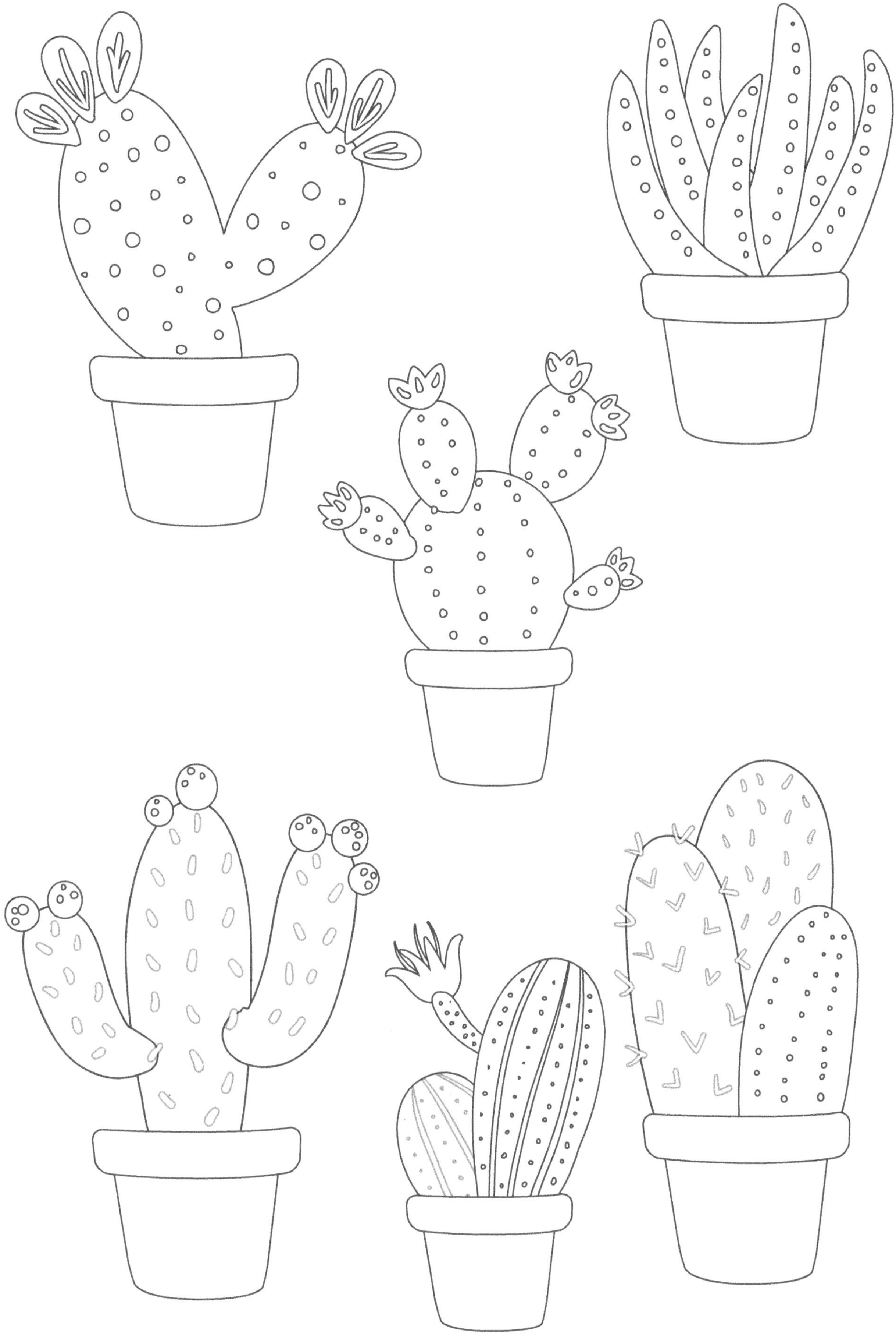

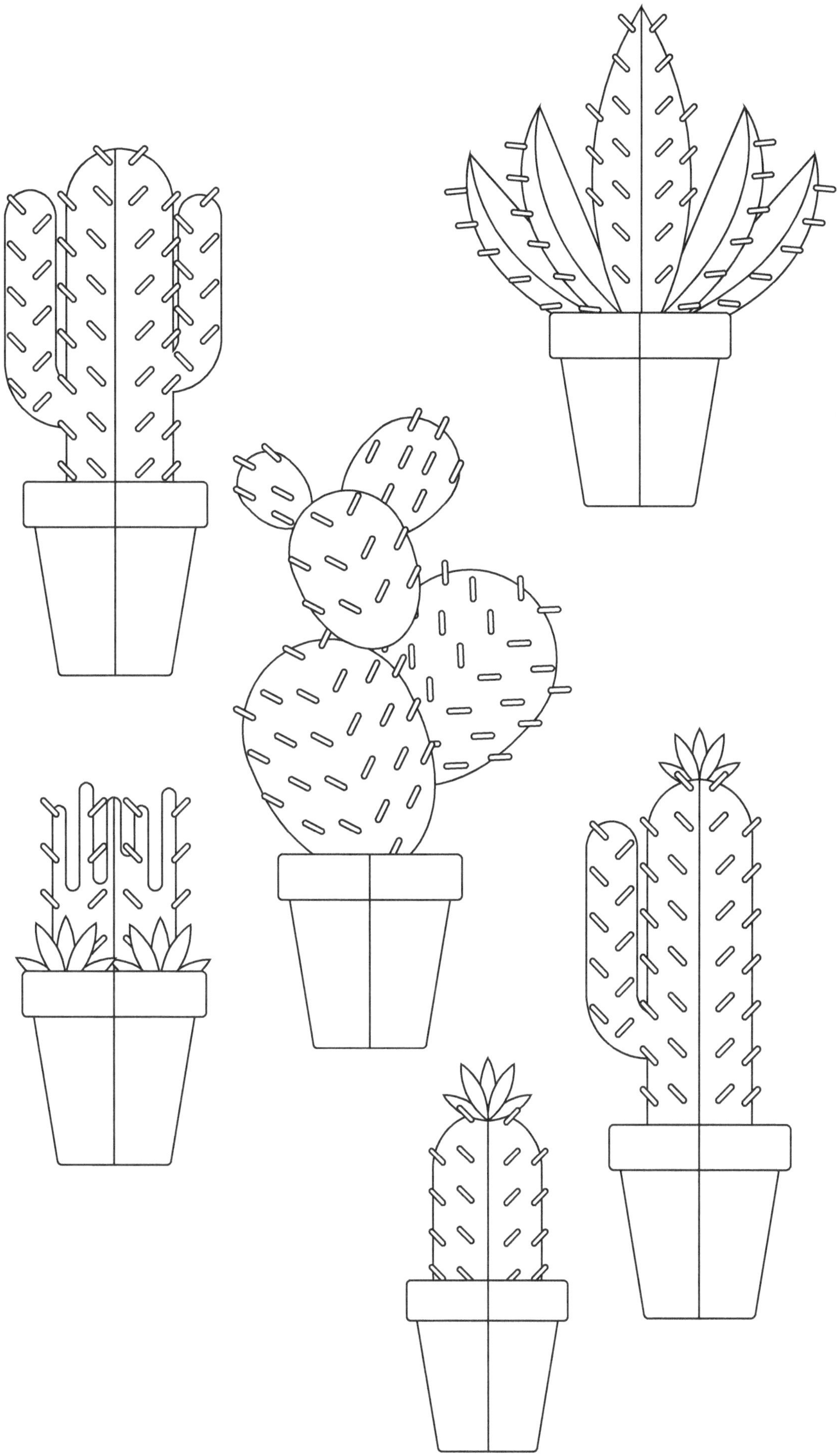

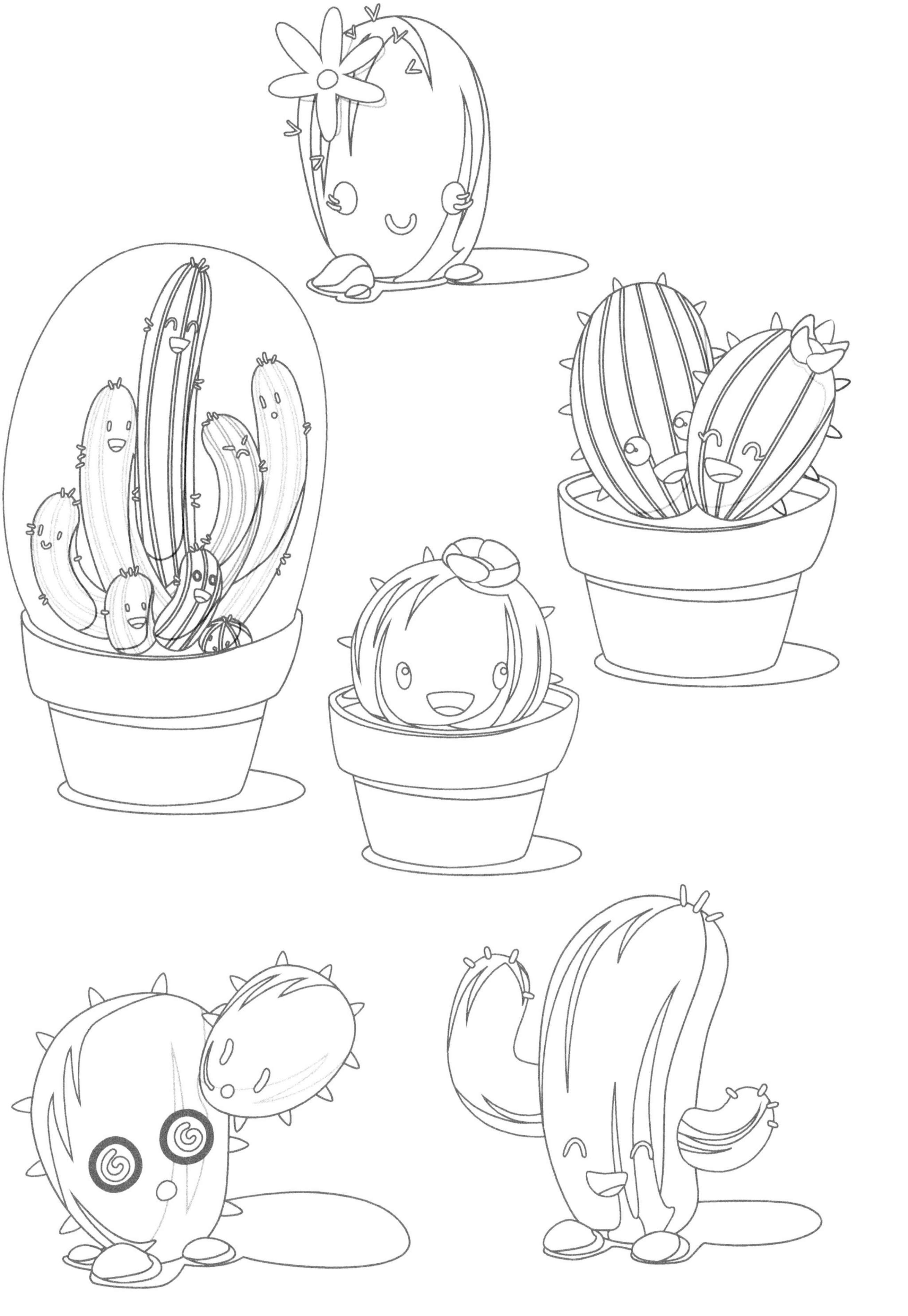

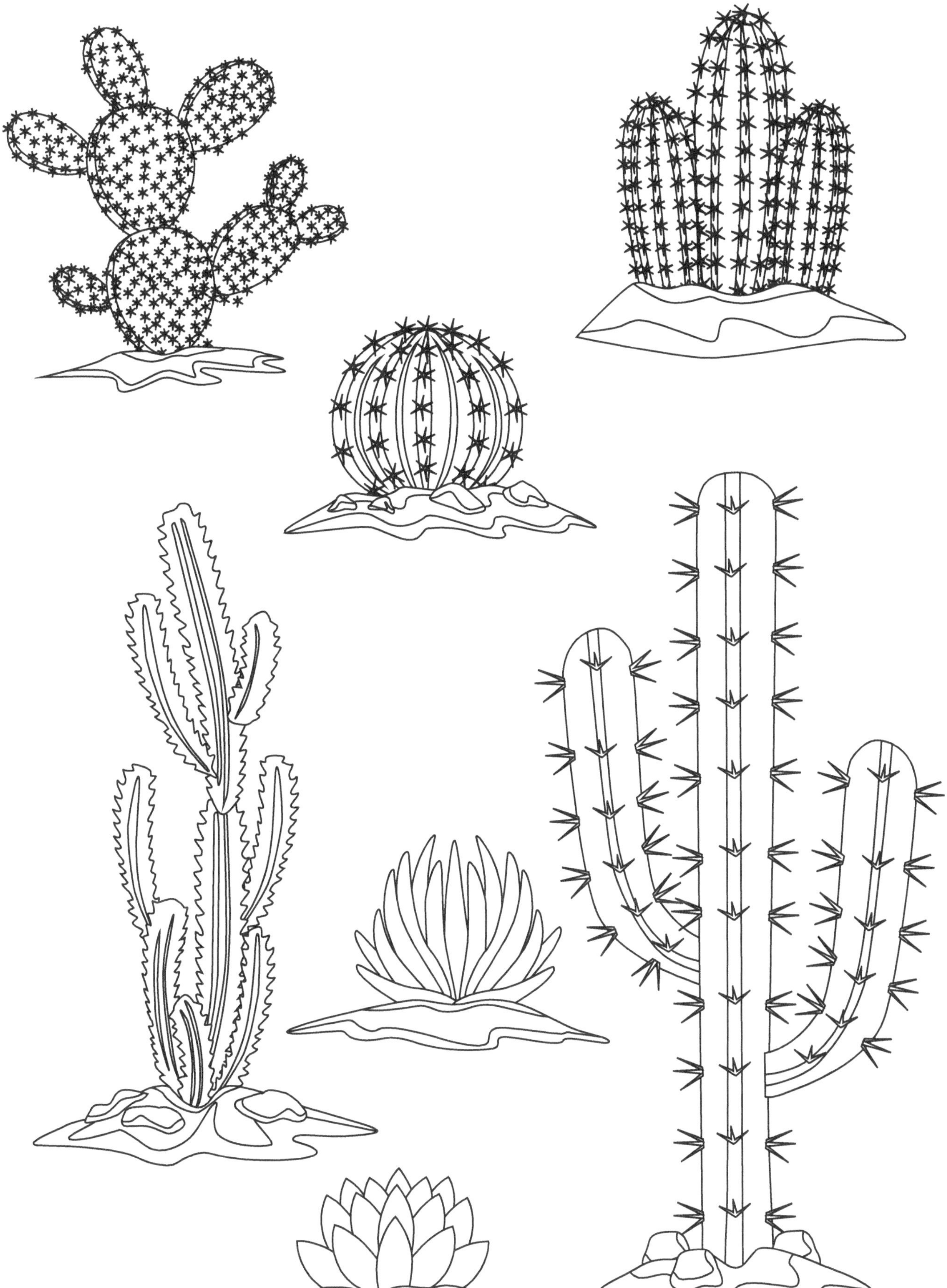

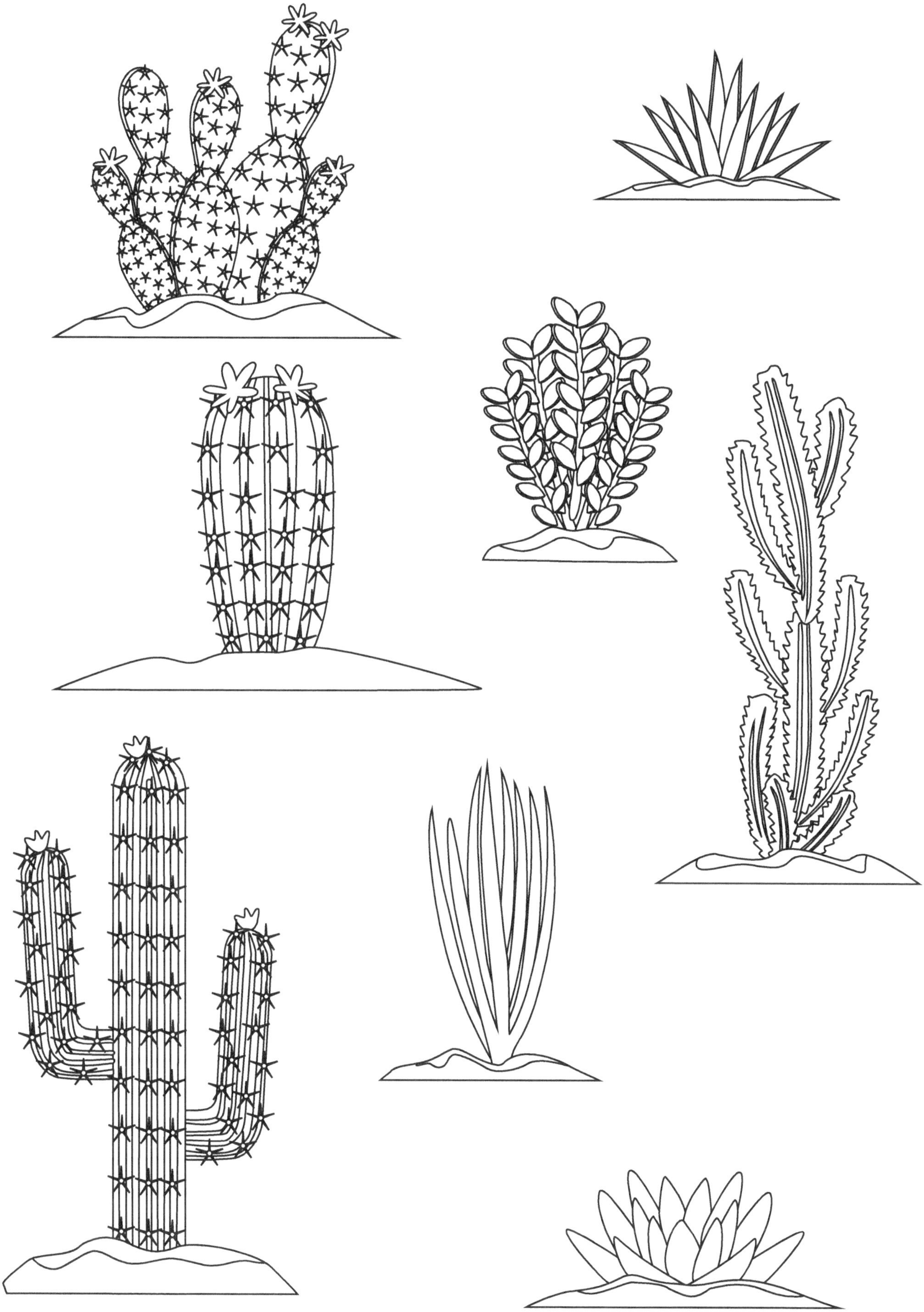

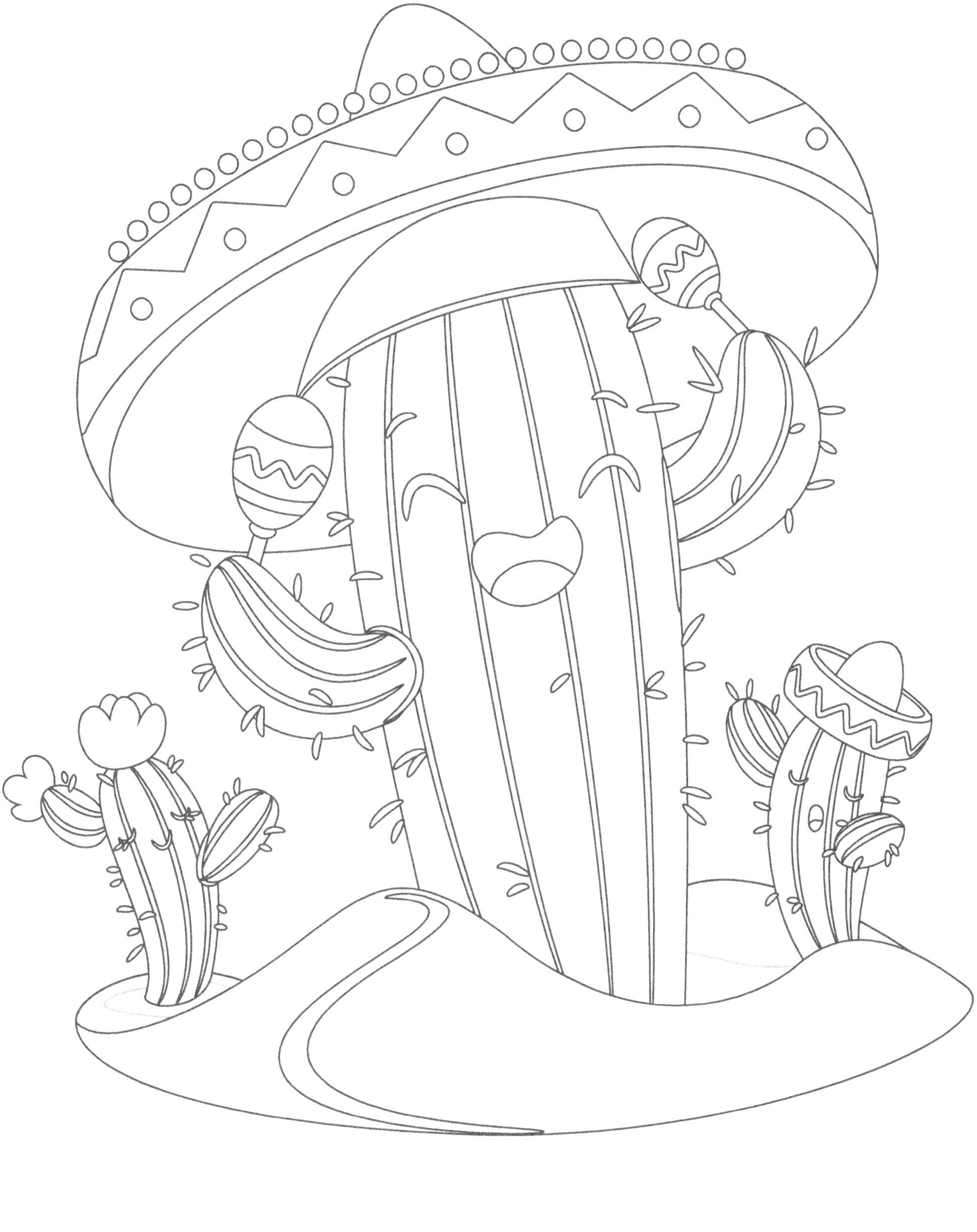

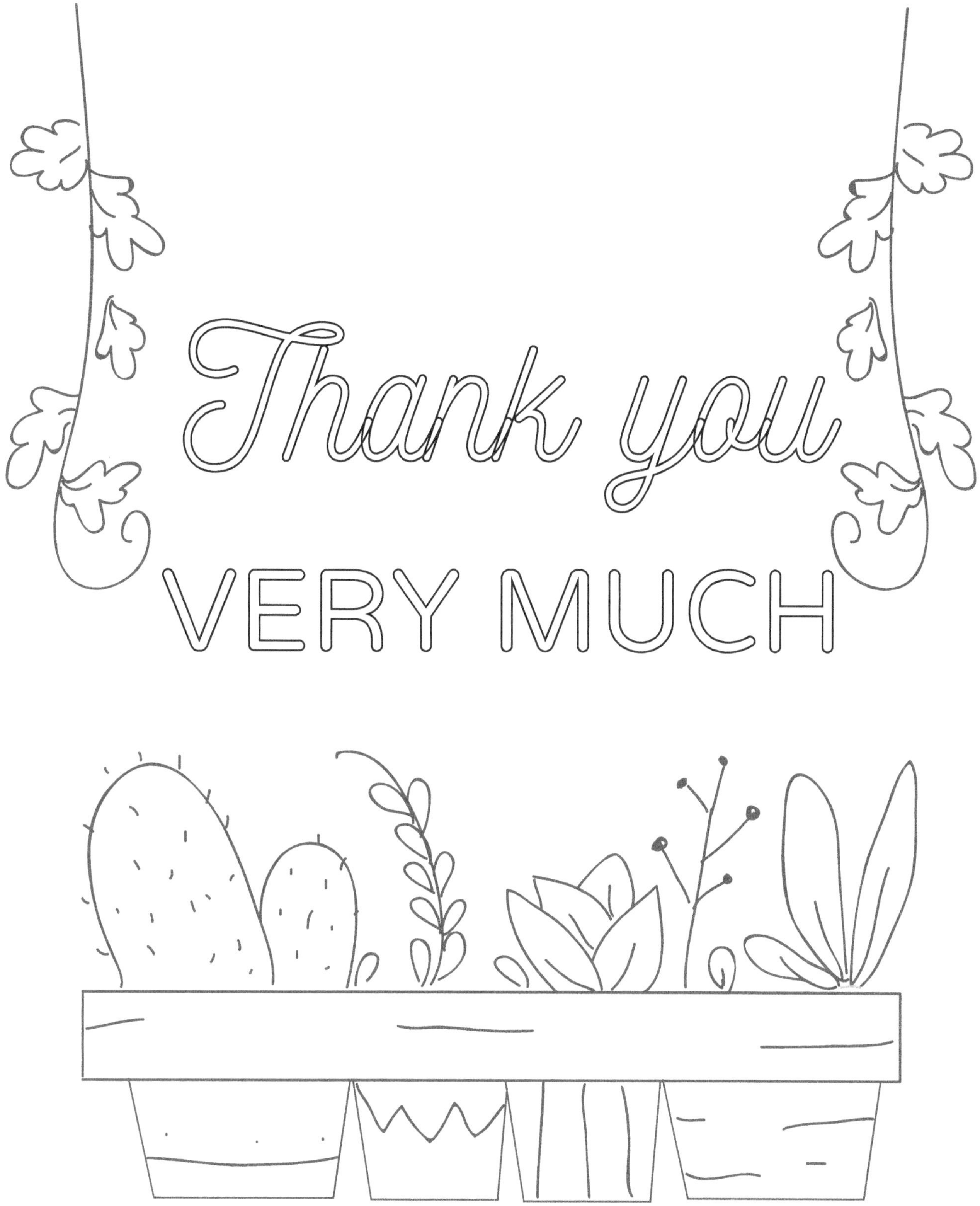
Thank you
VERY MUCH

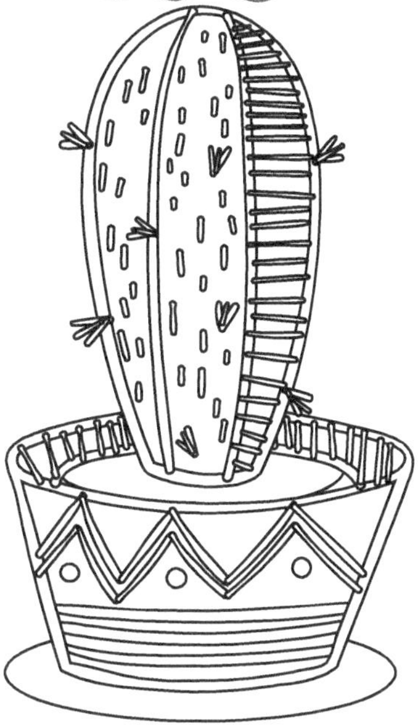

Thank you

FOR EVERYTHING

Thank you

FOR THE THINGS YOU'VE DONE

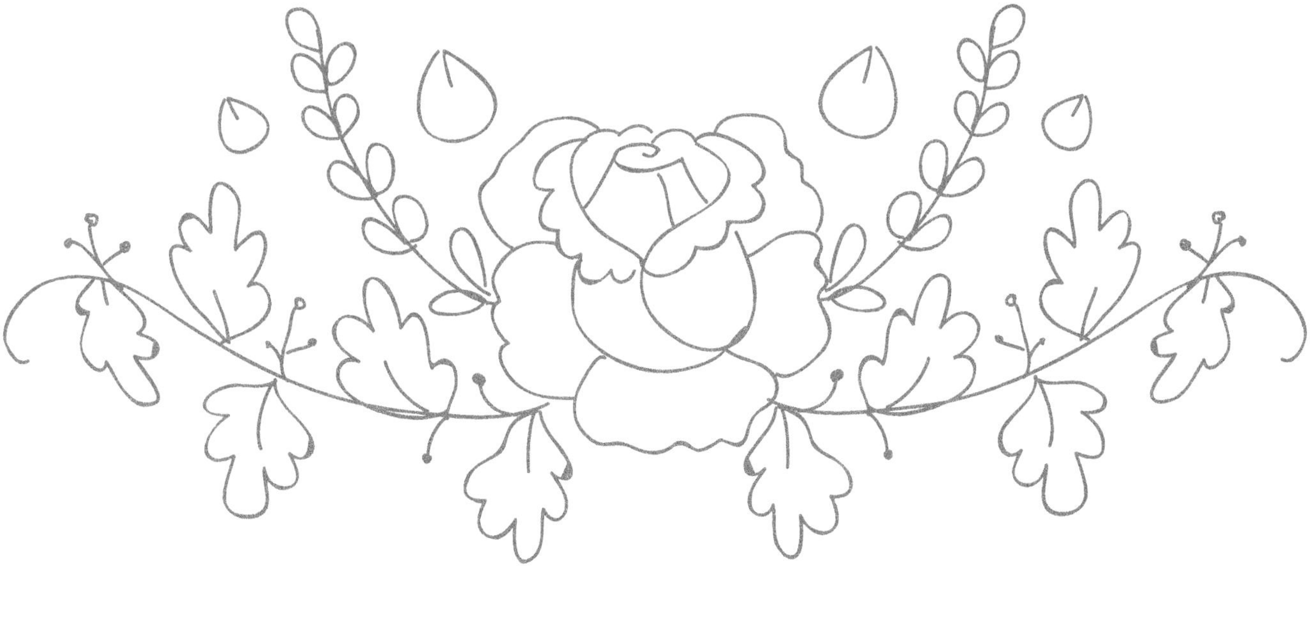

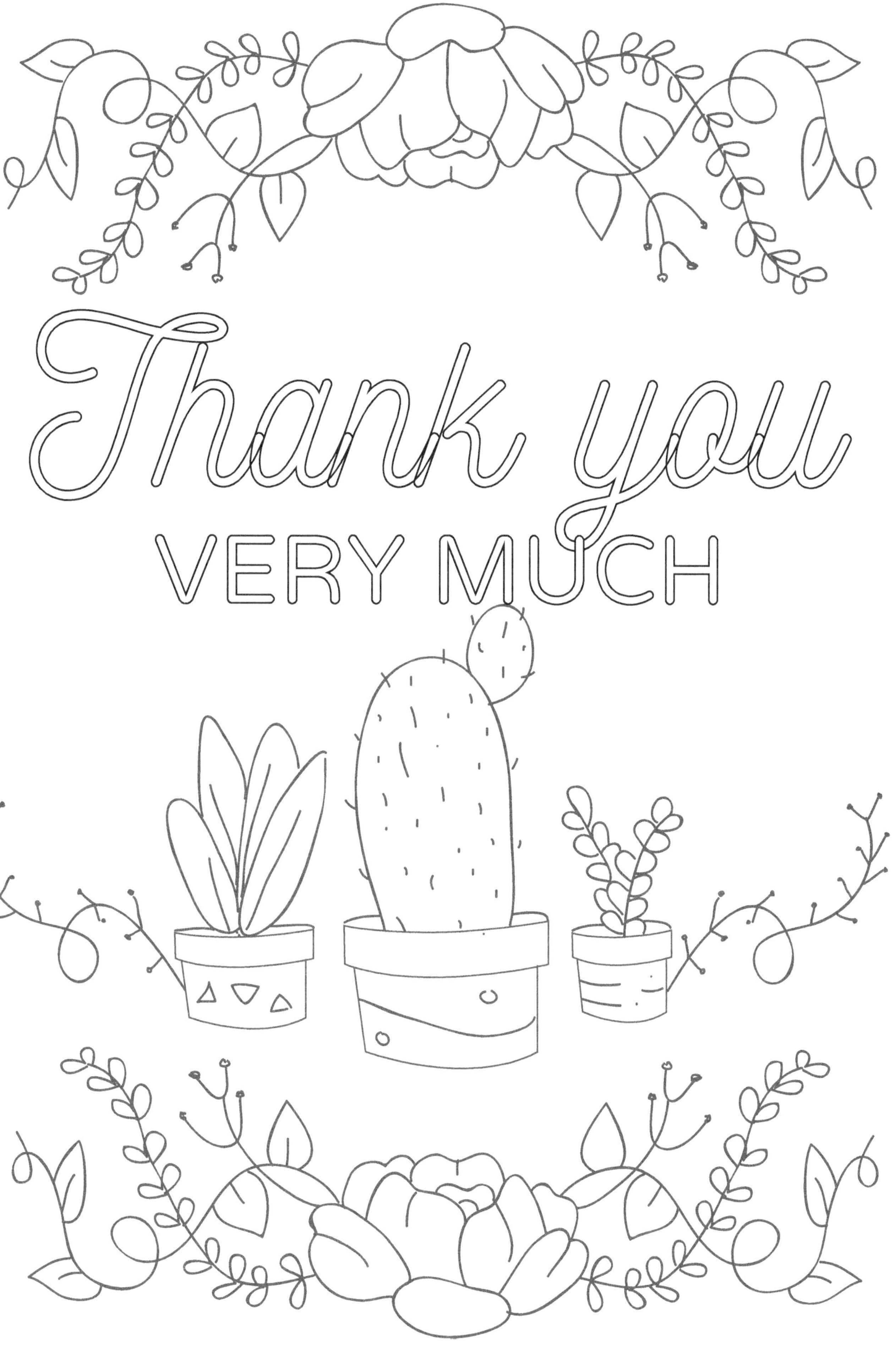
Thank you
VERY MUCH

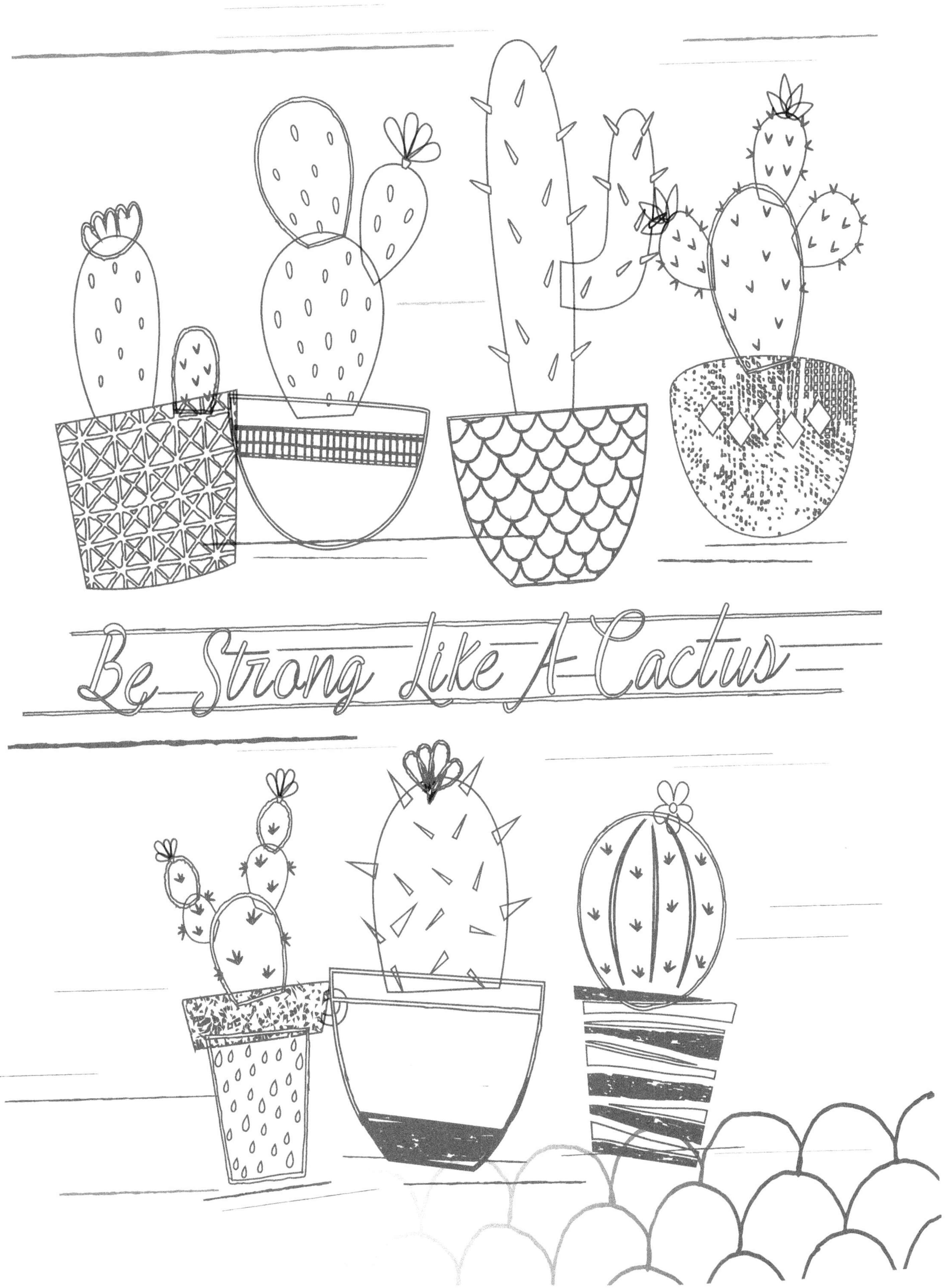
Be Strong Like A Cactus

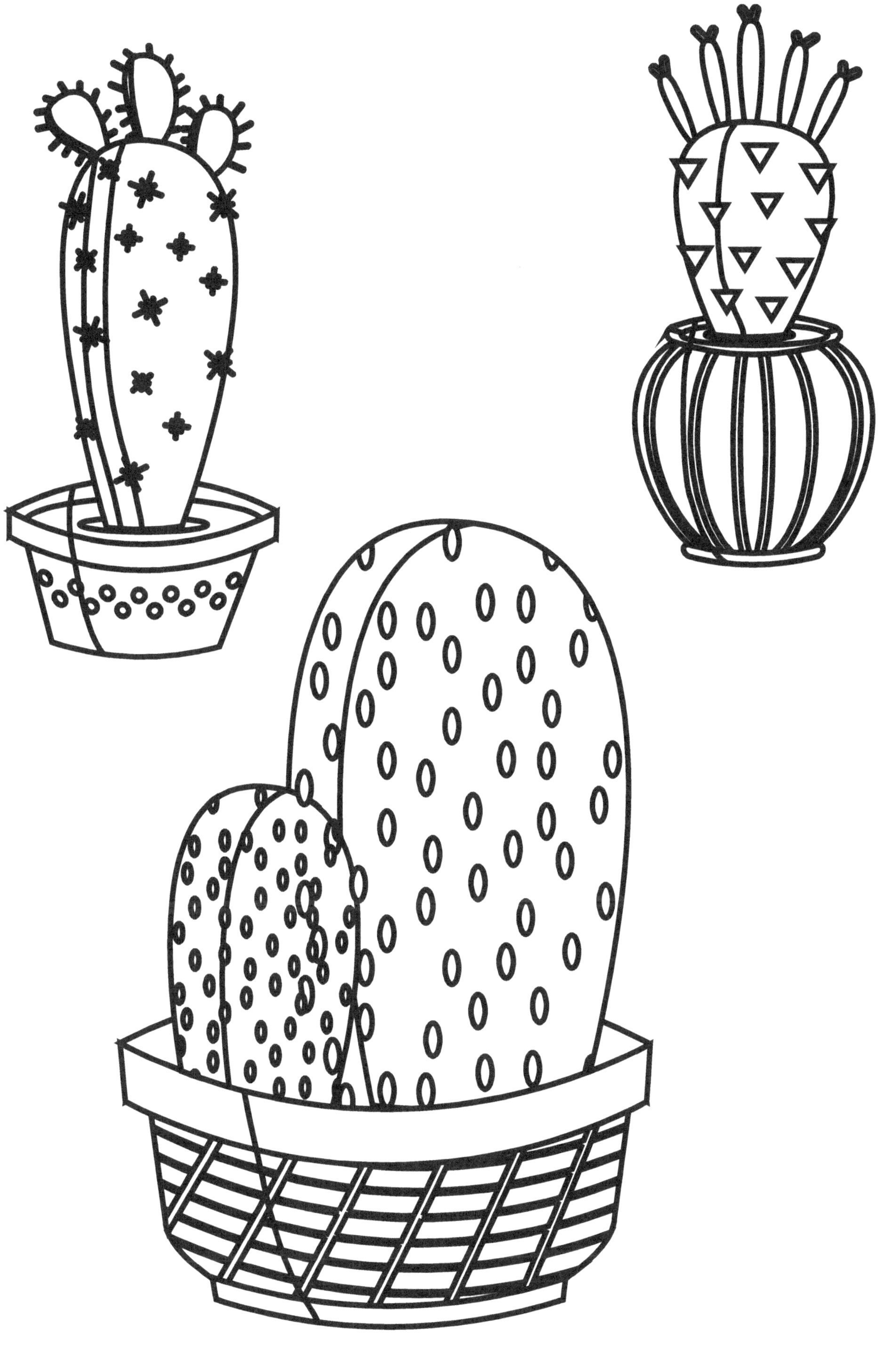

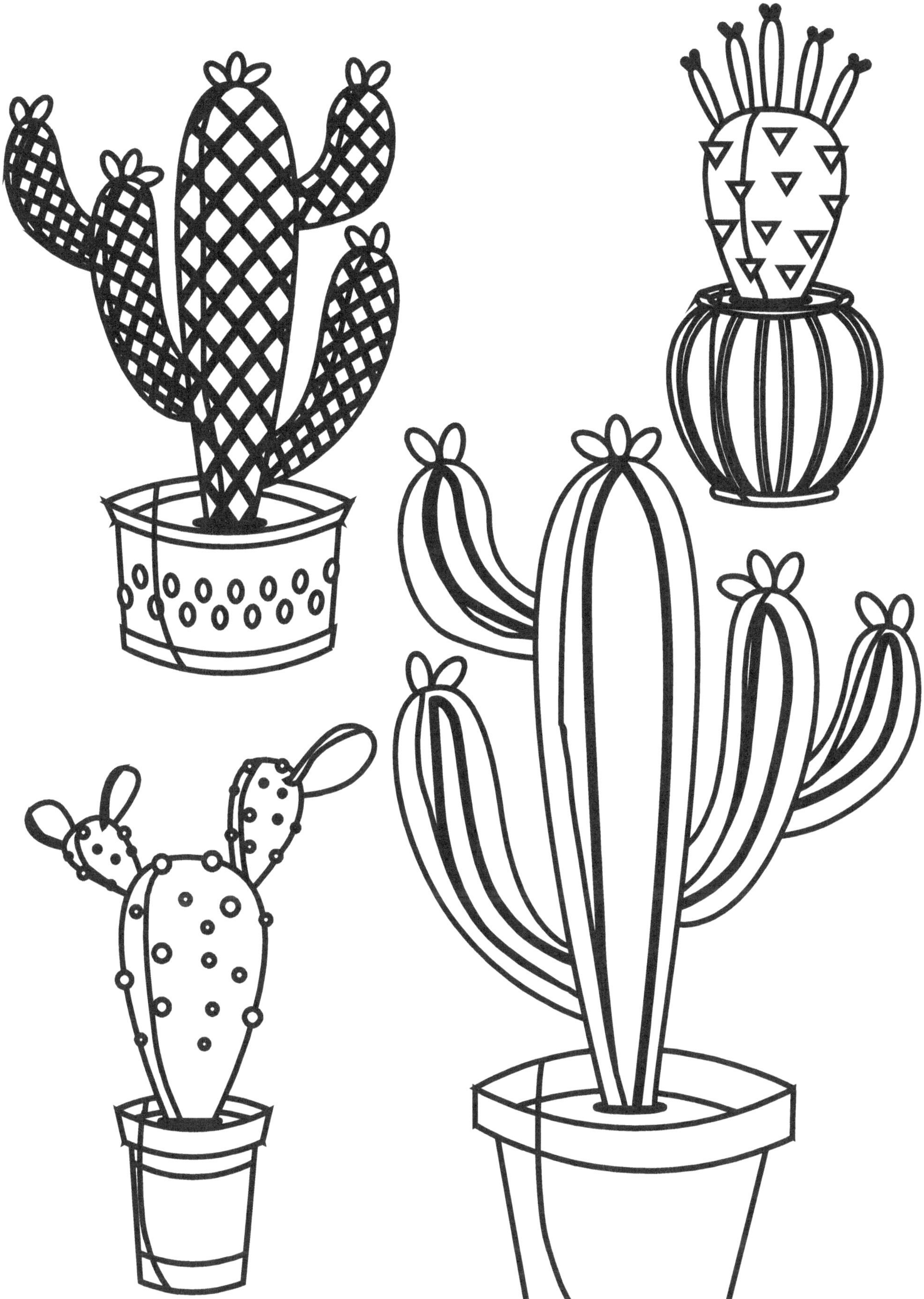

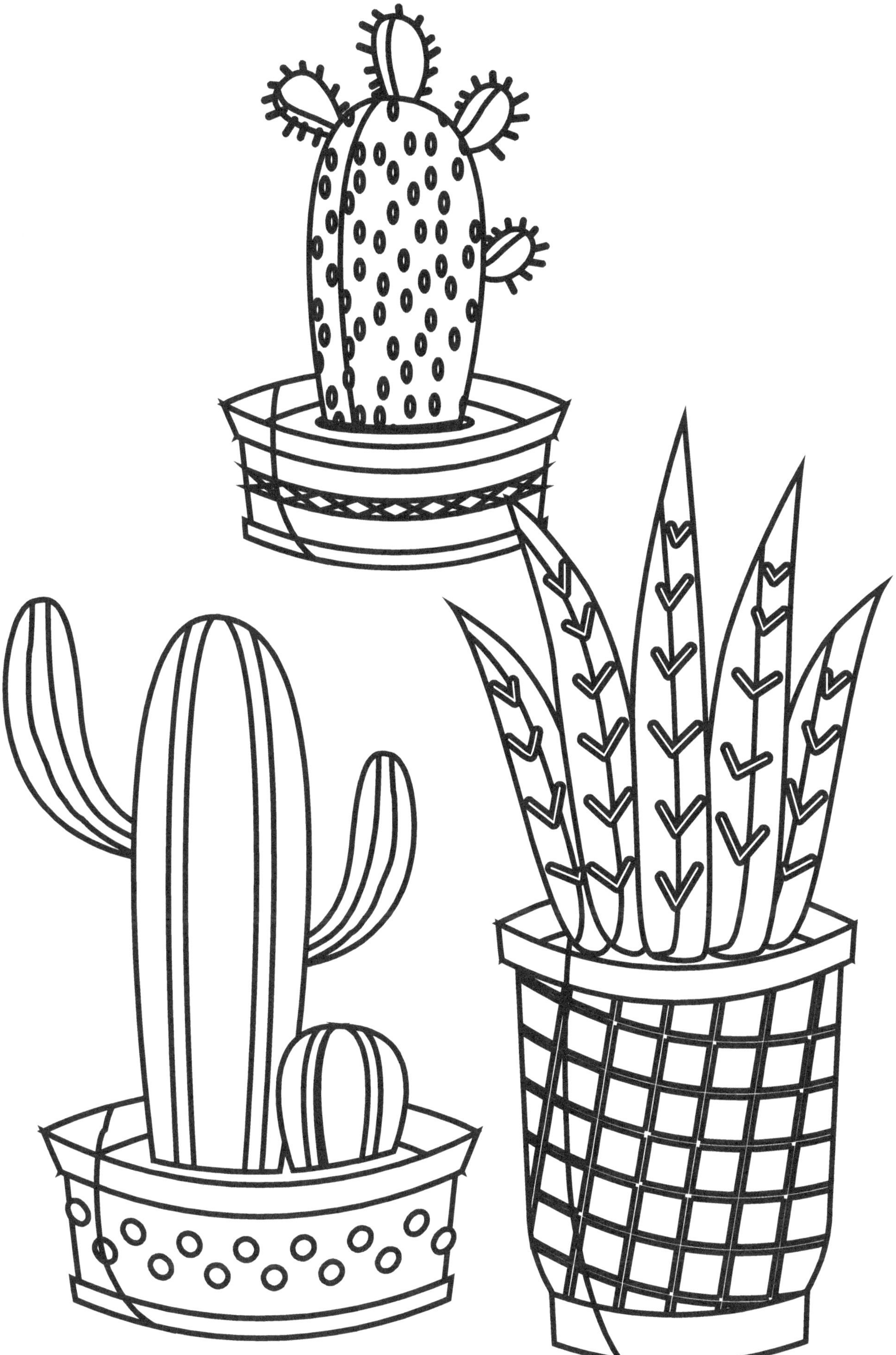

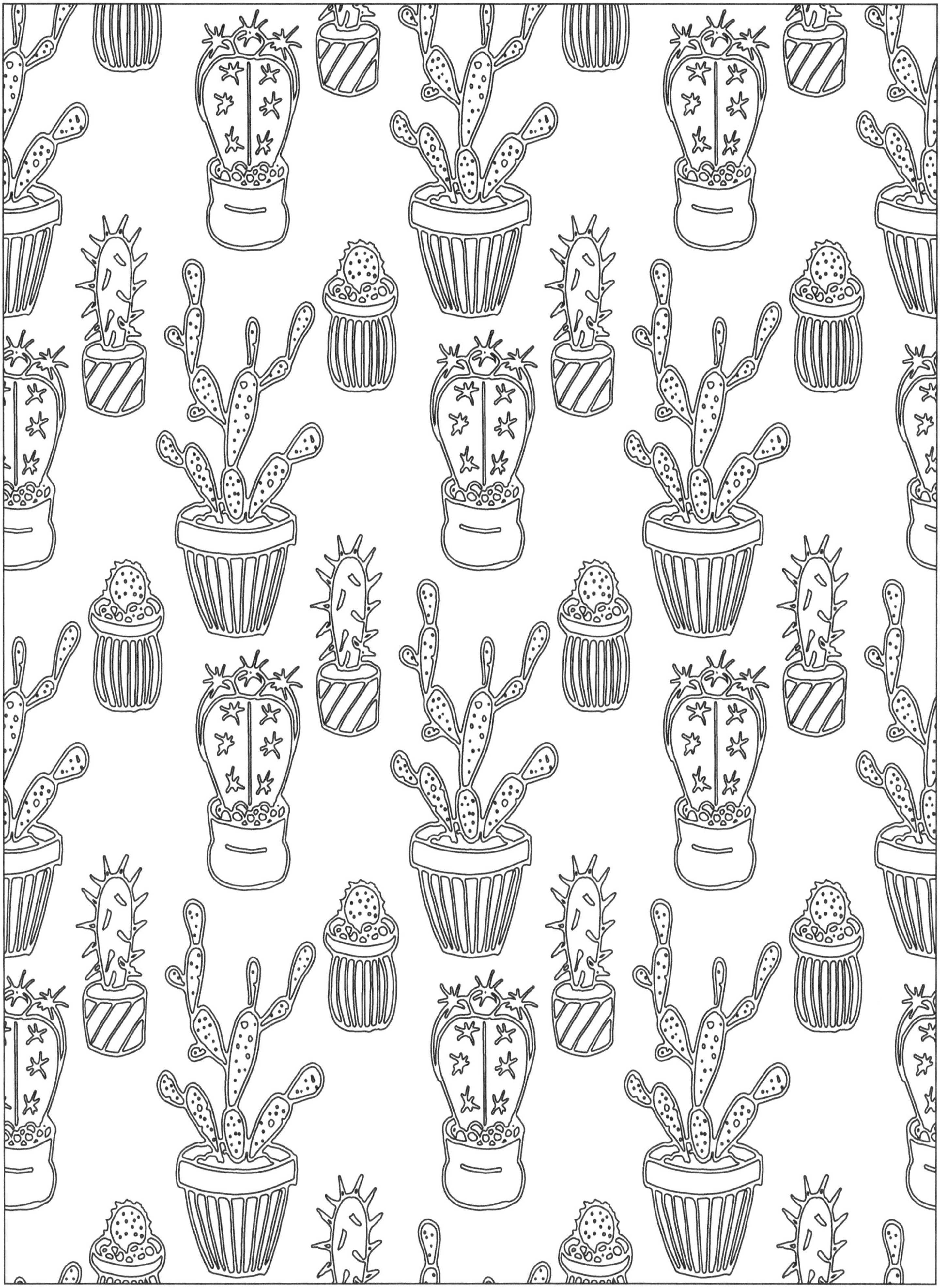

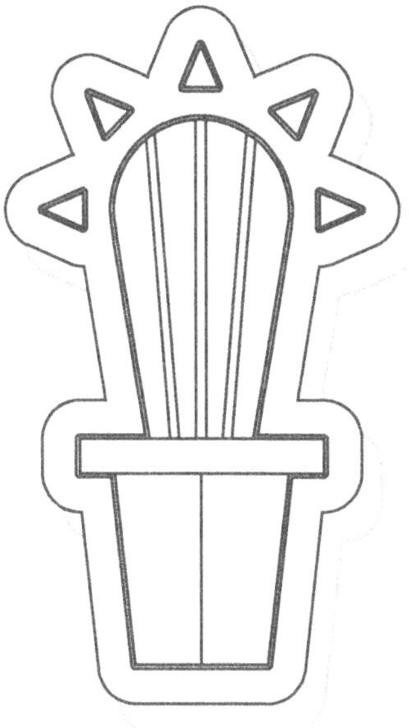
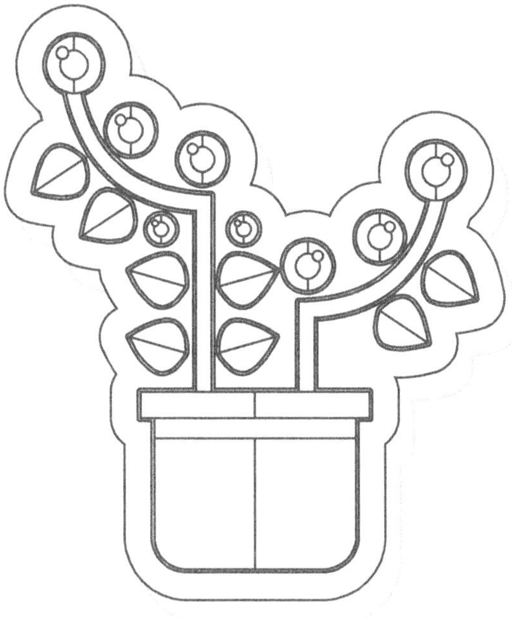
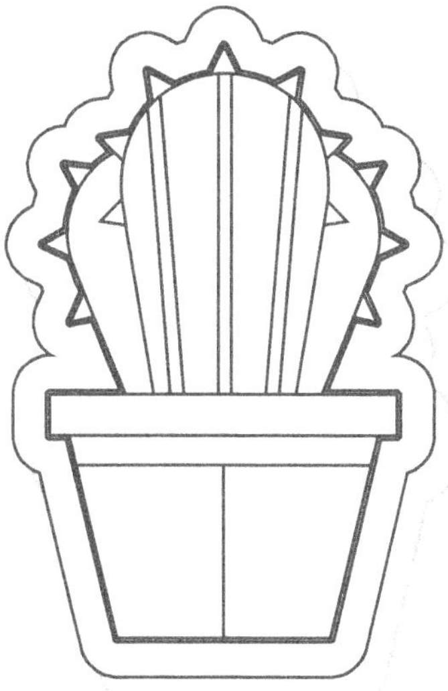
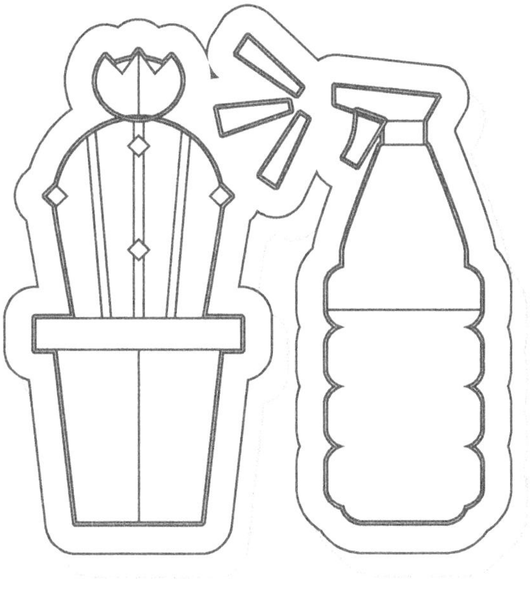
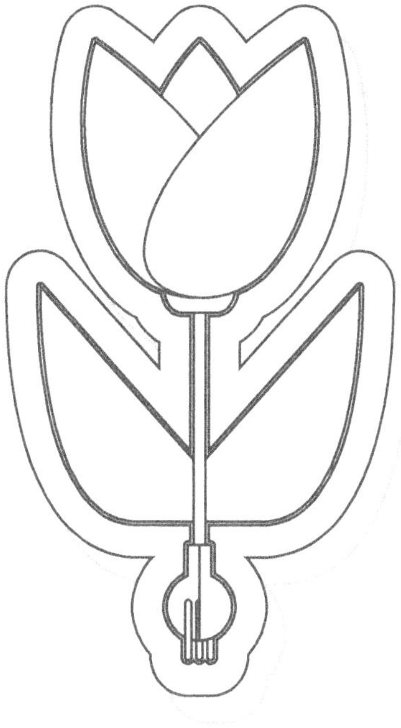
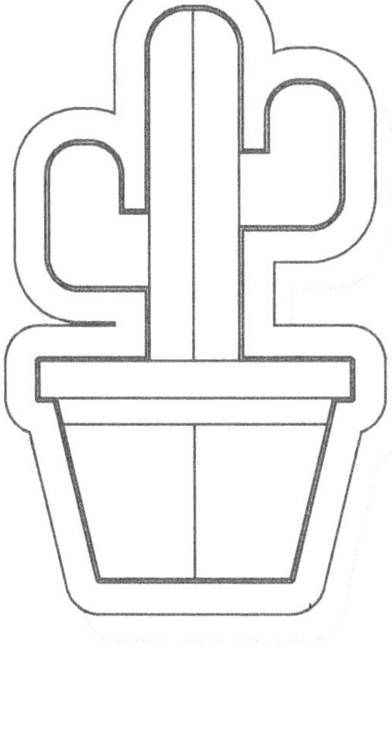
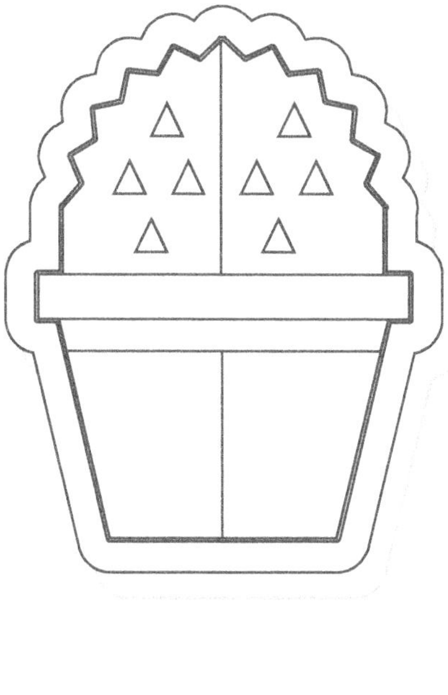

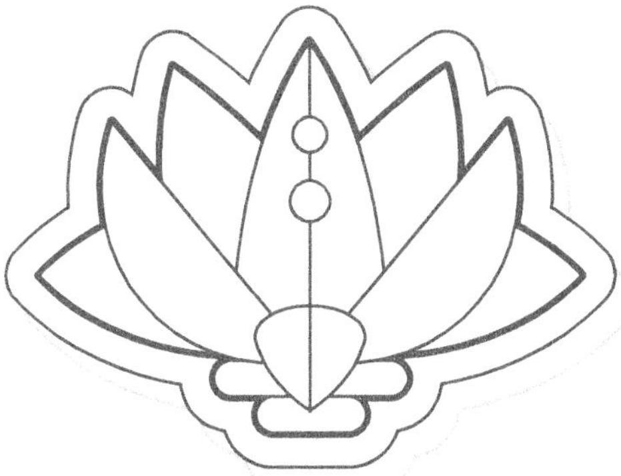
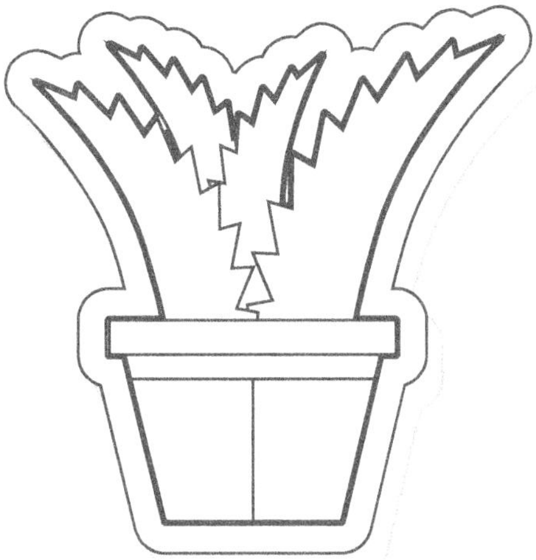
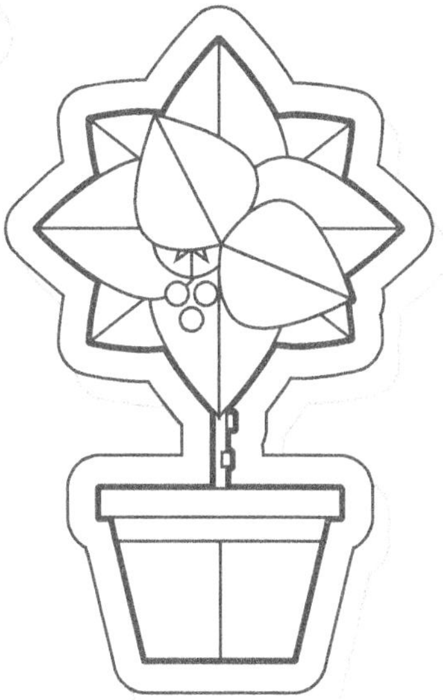
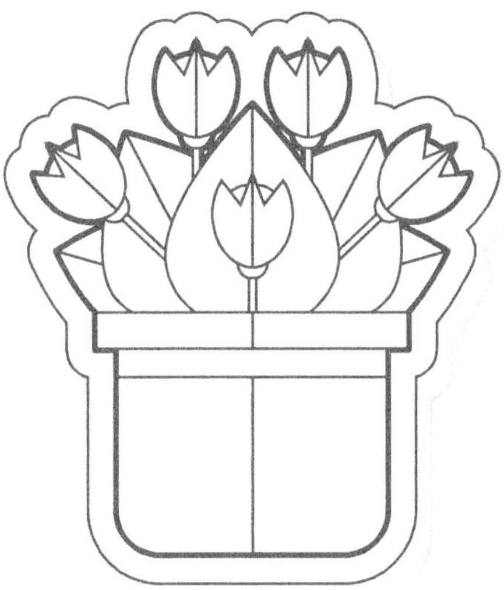
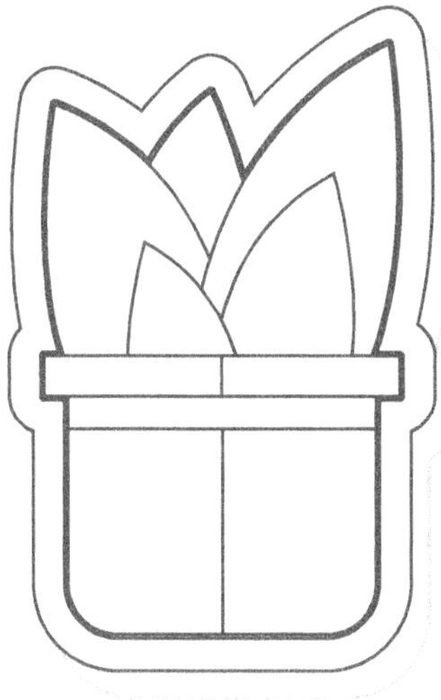

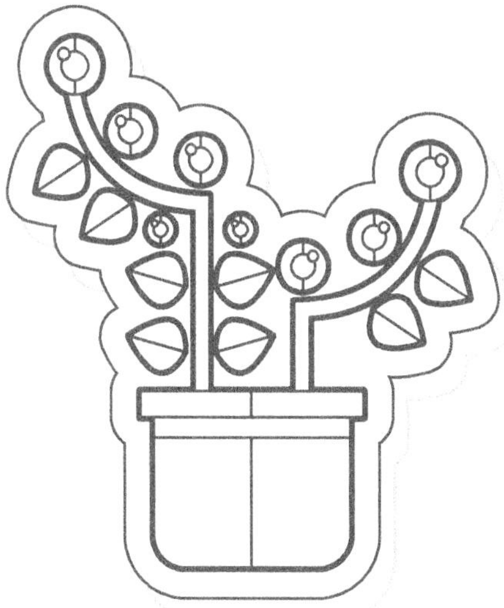

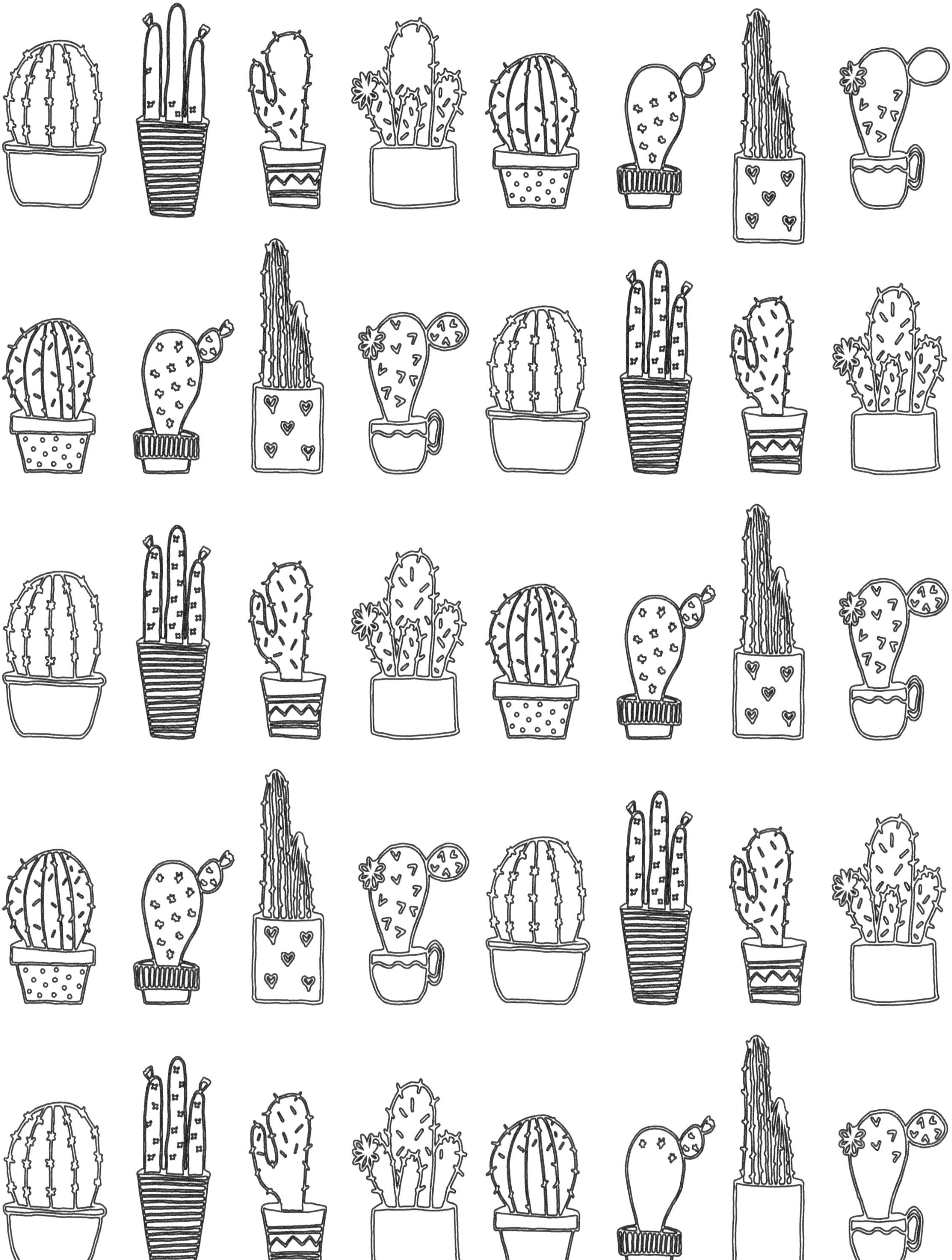

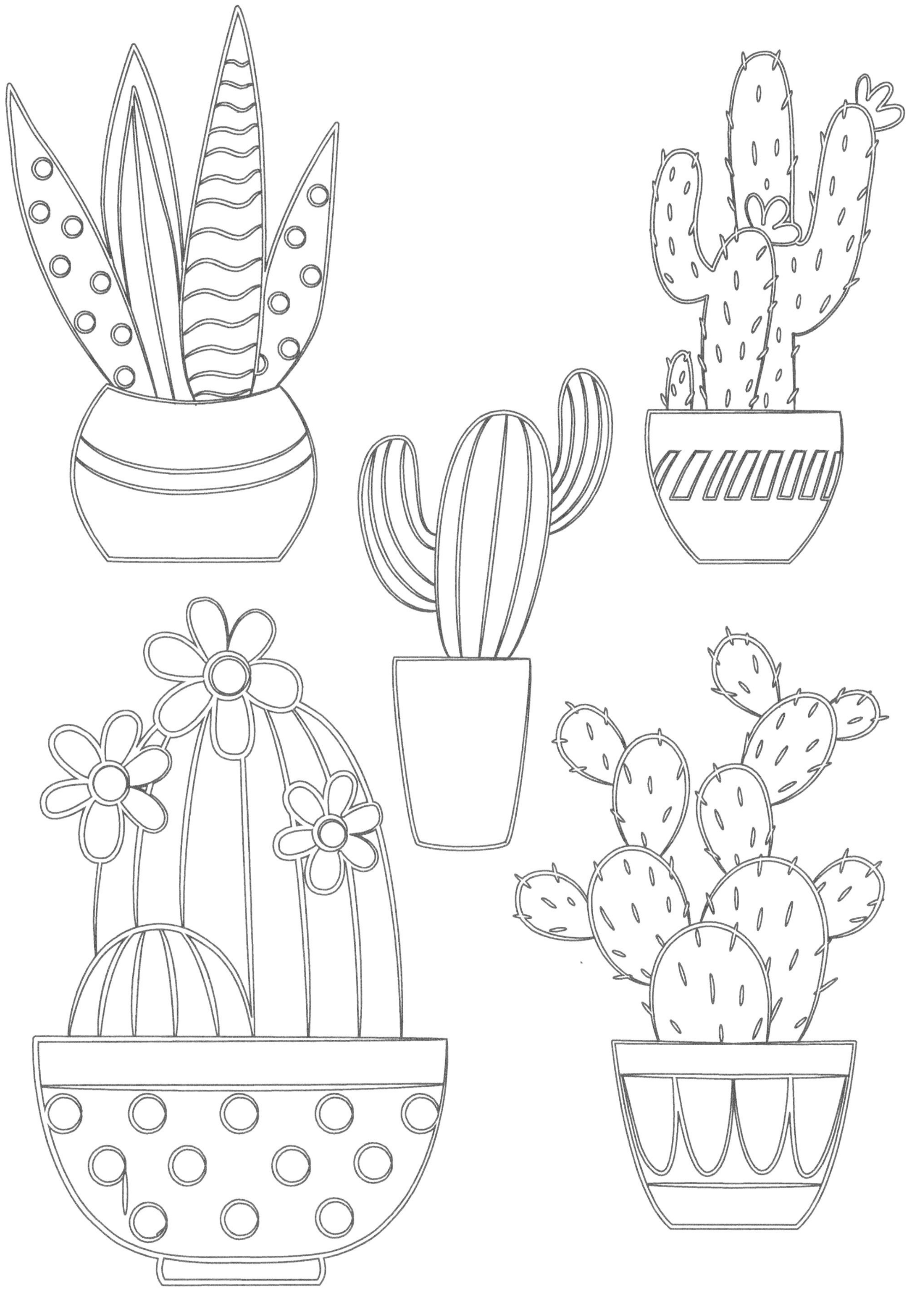

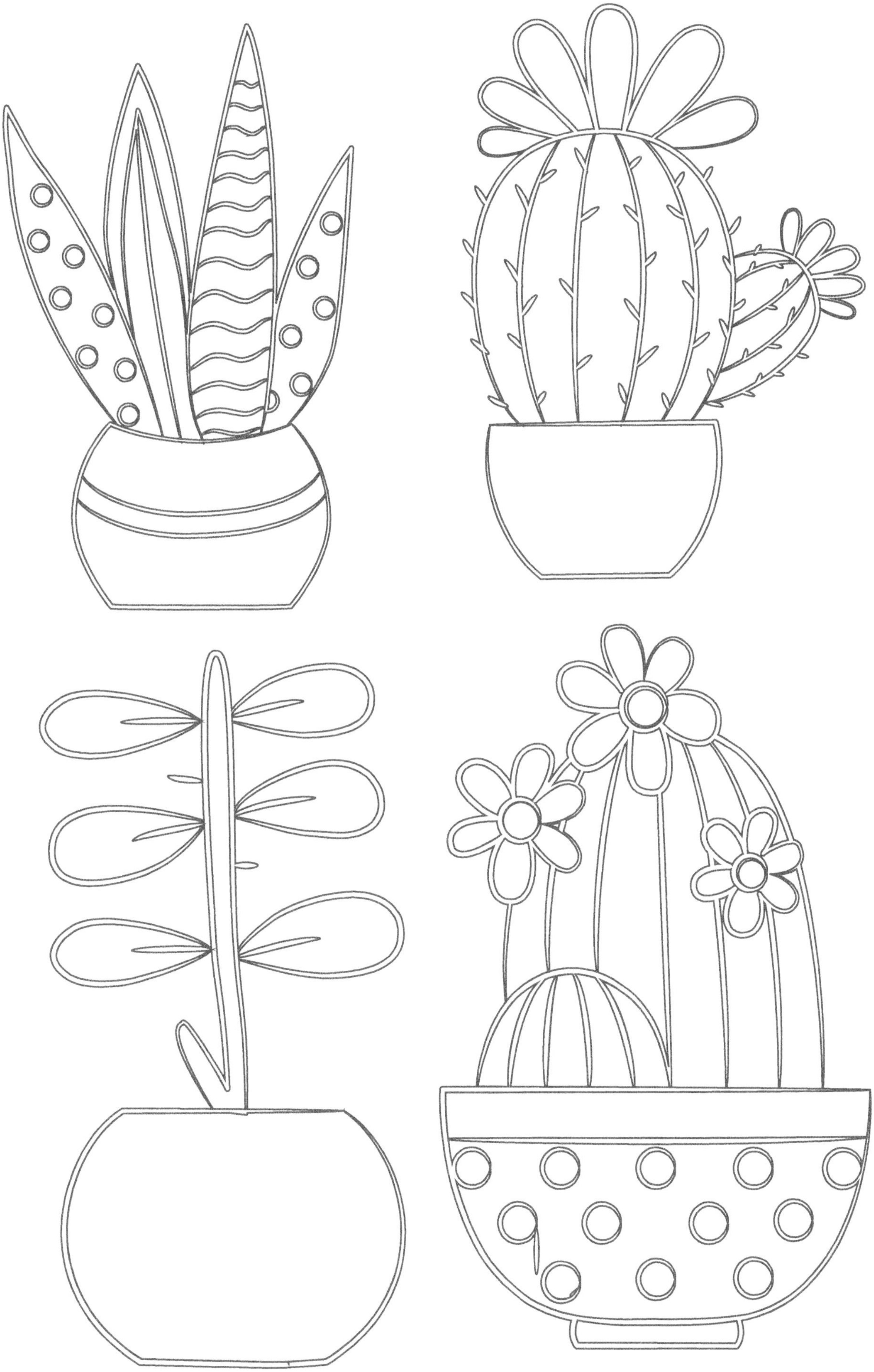

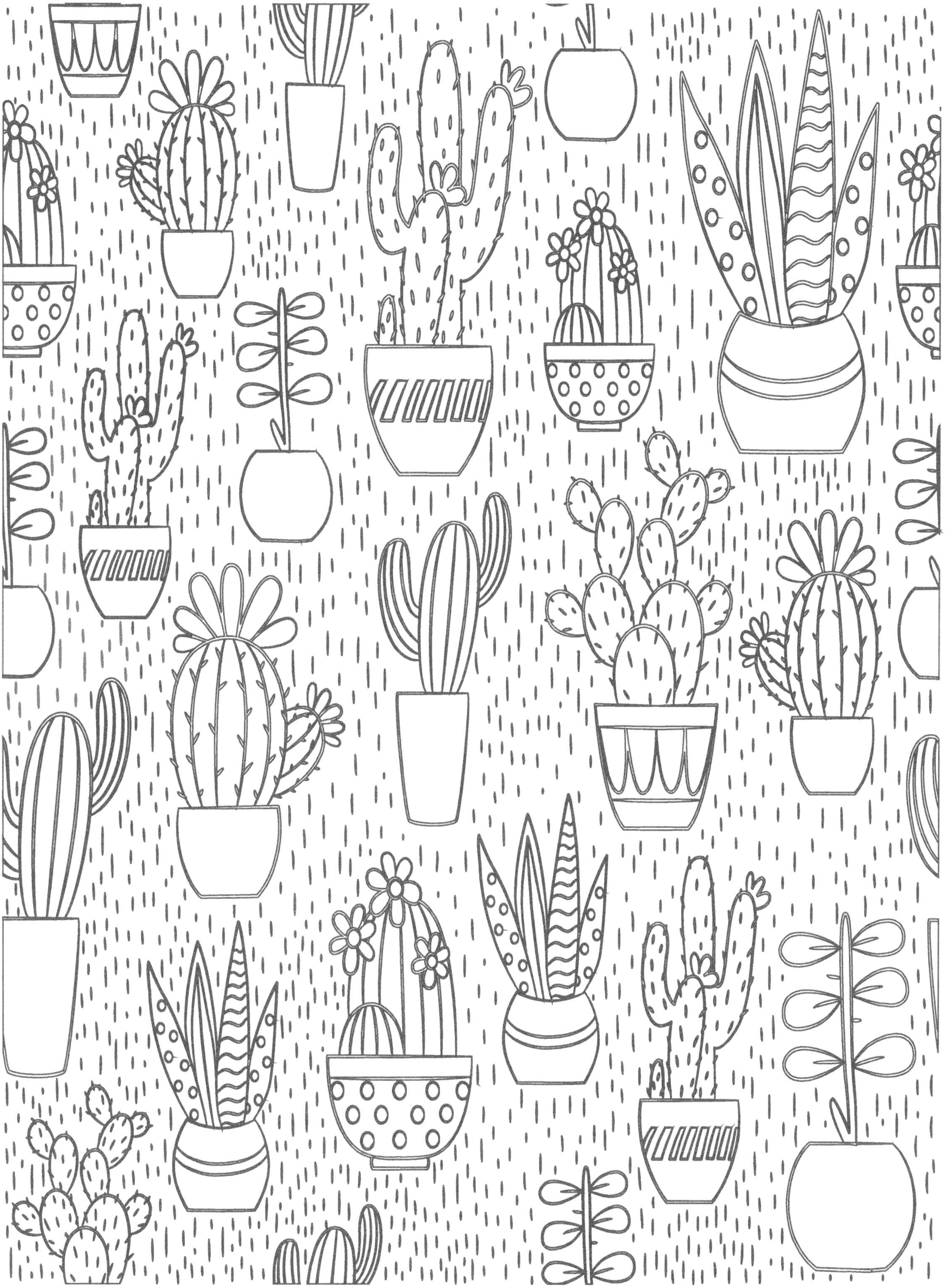

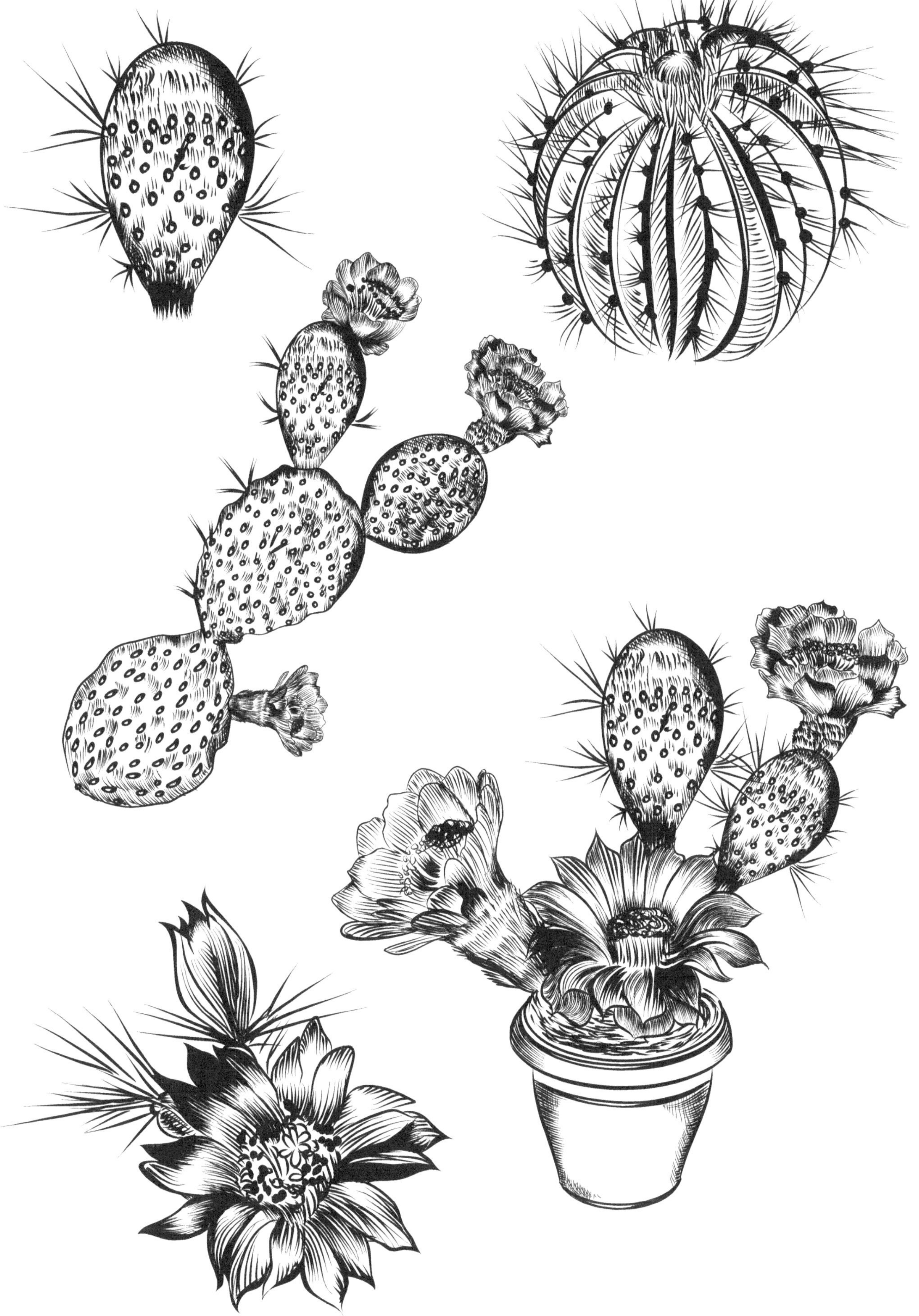

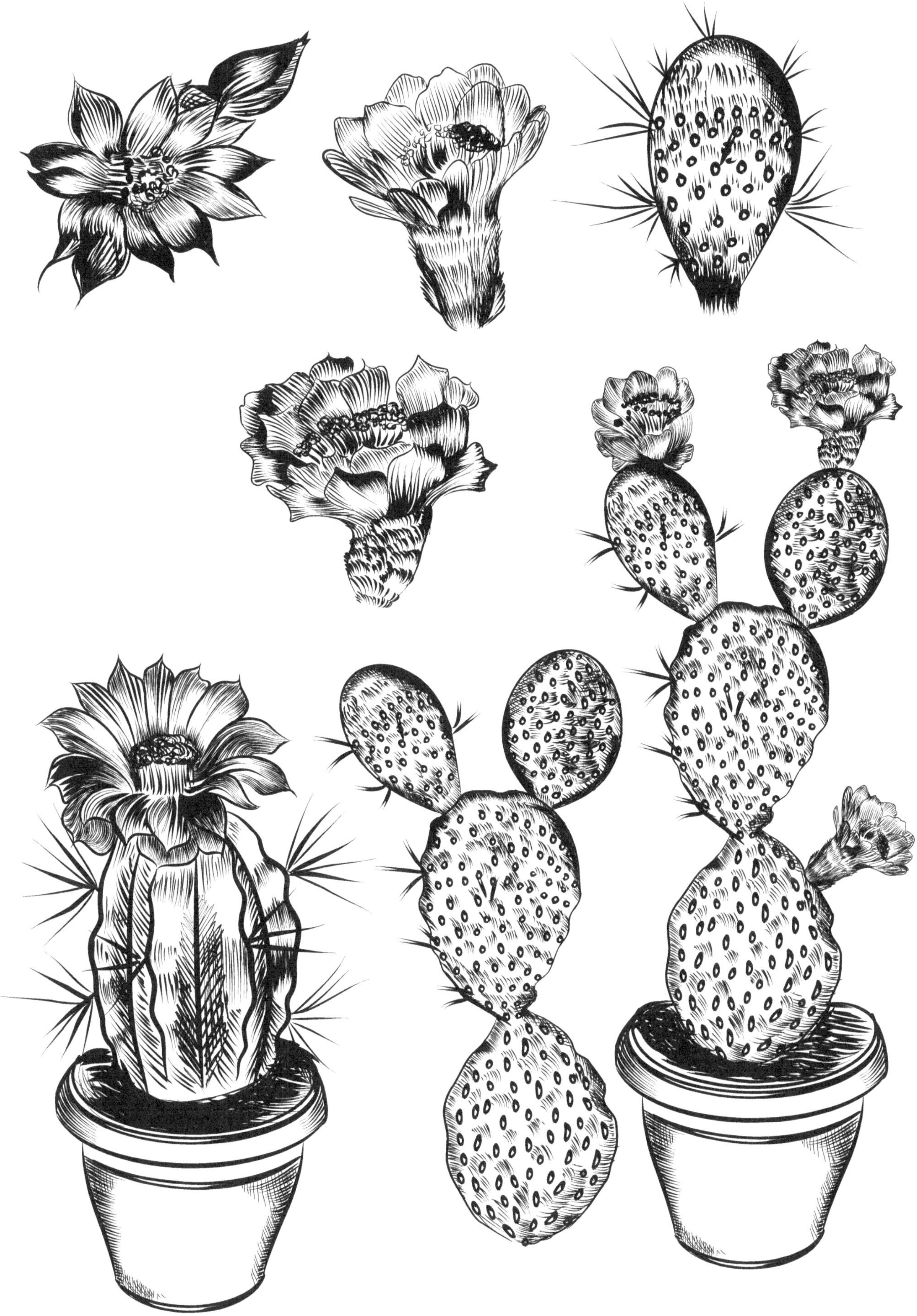

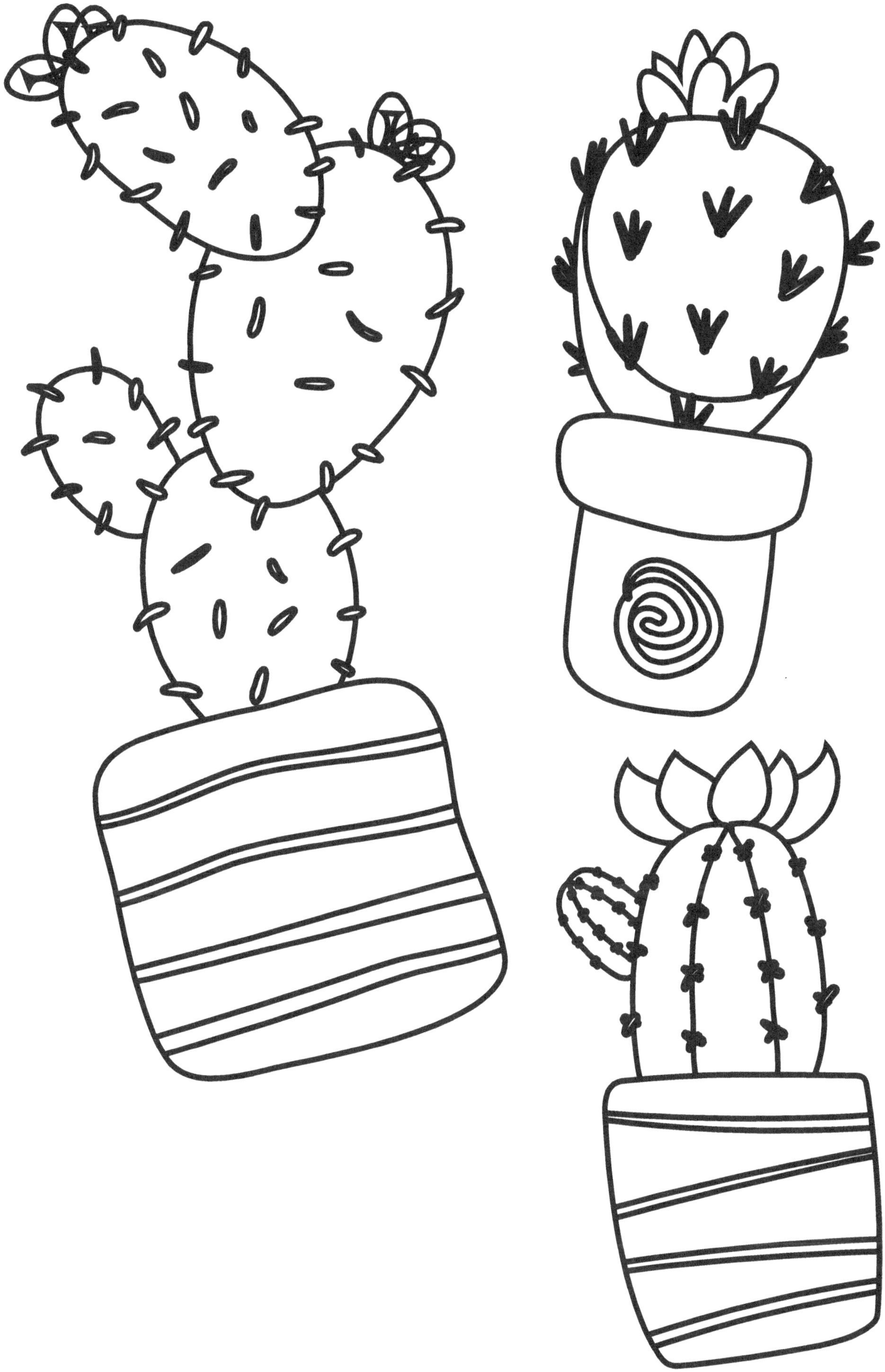

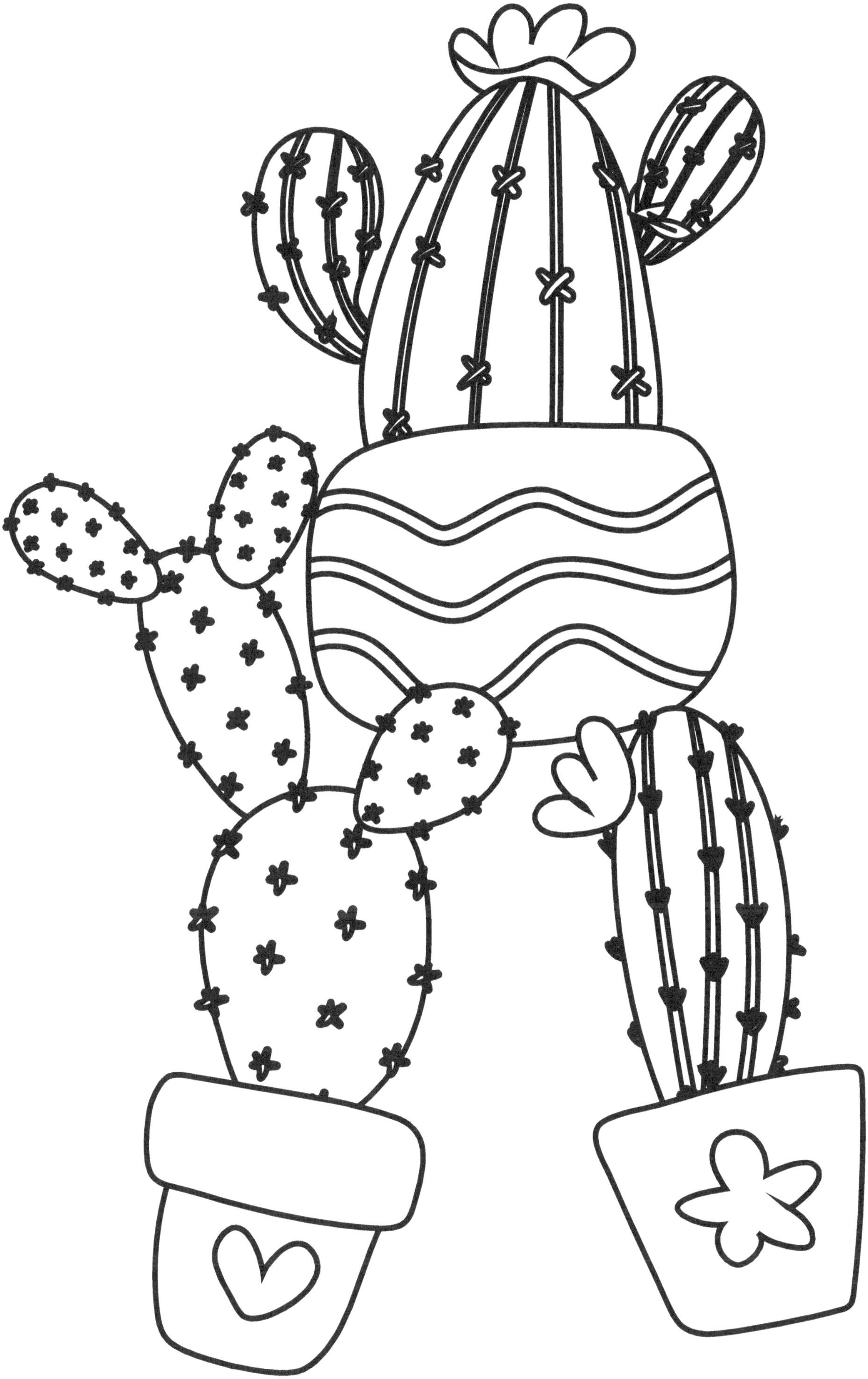

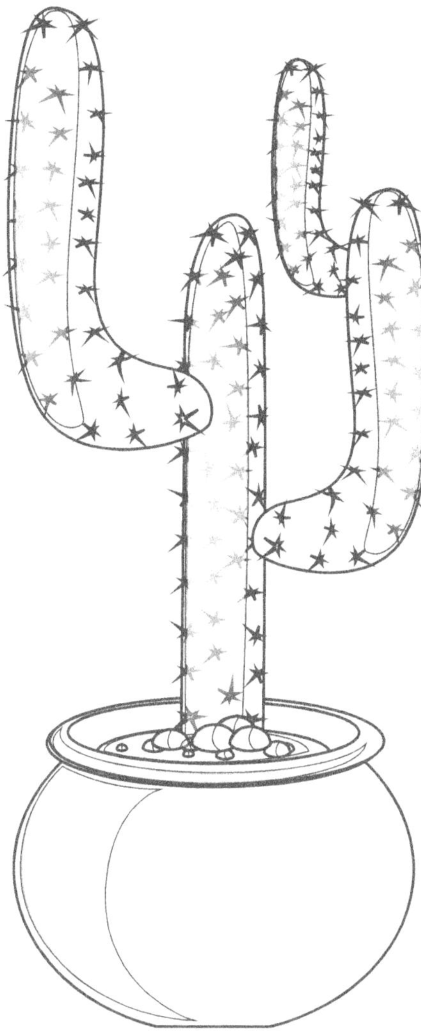
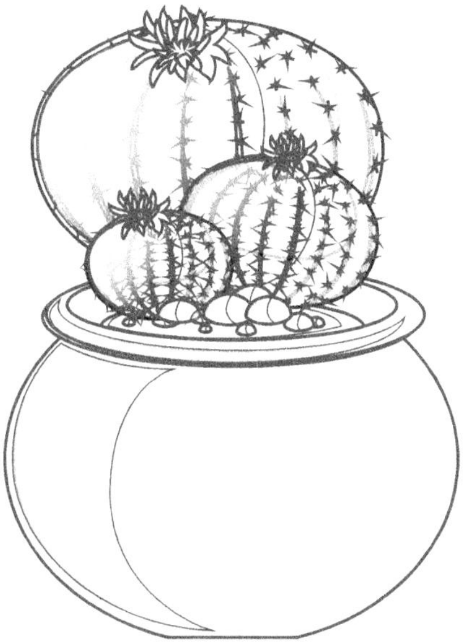
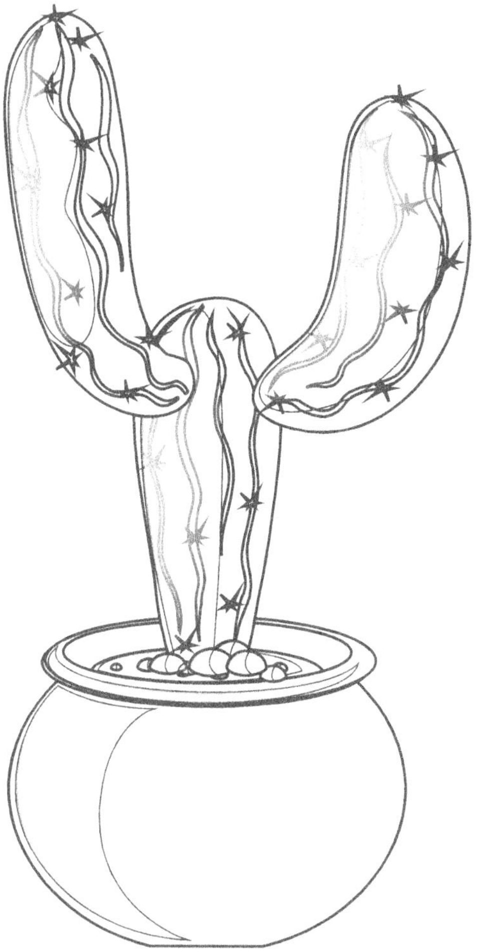
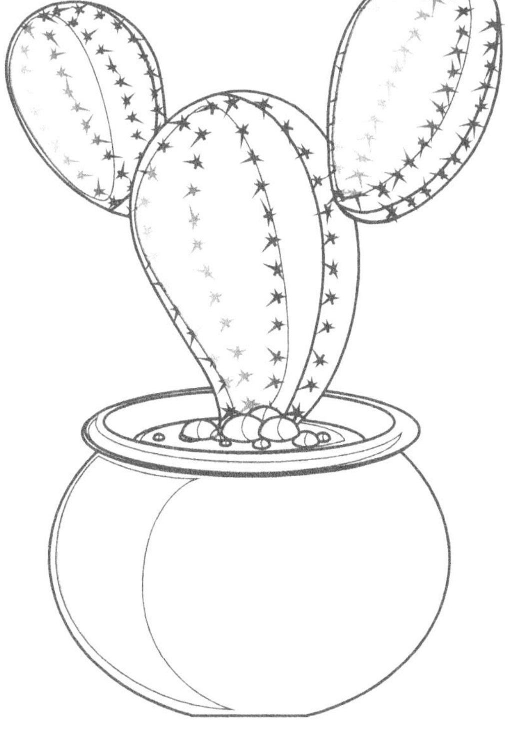
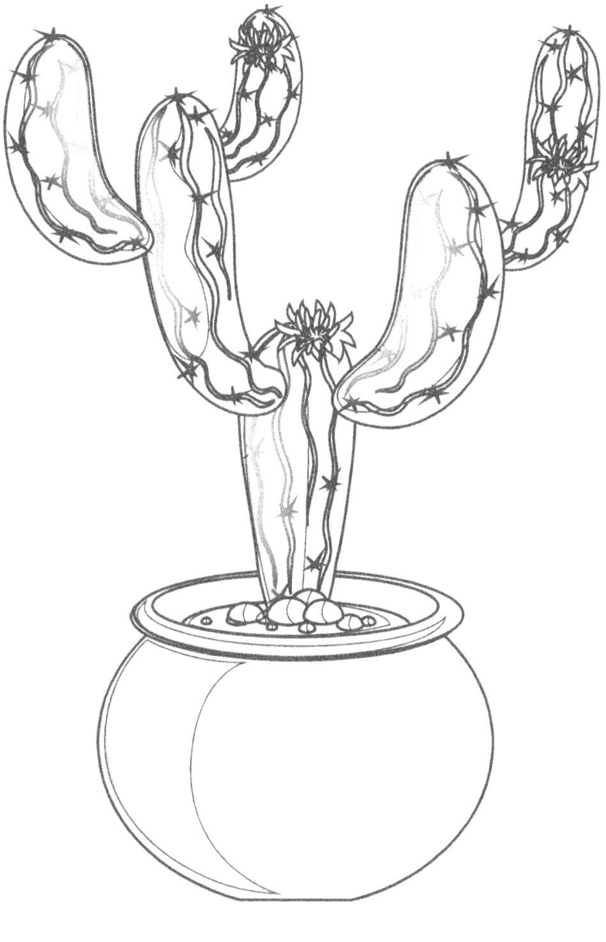

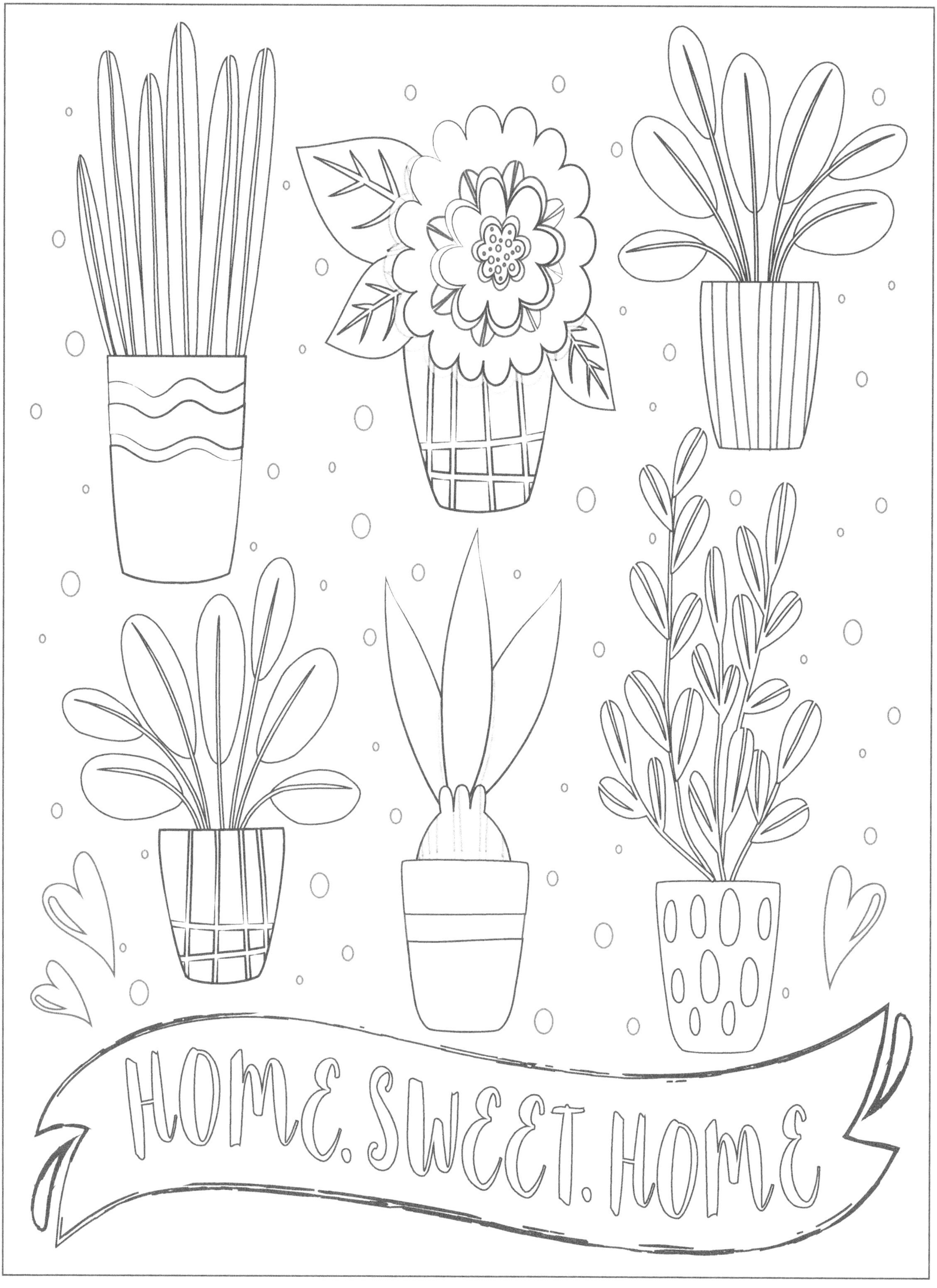
HOME. SWEET. HOME

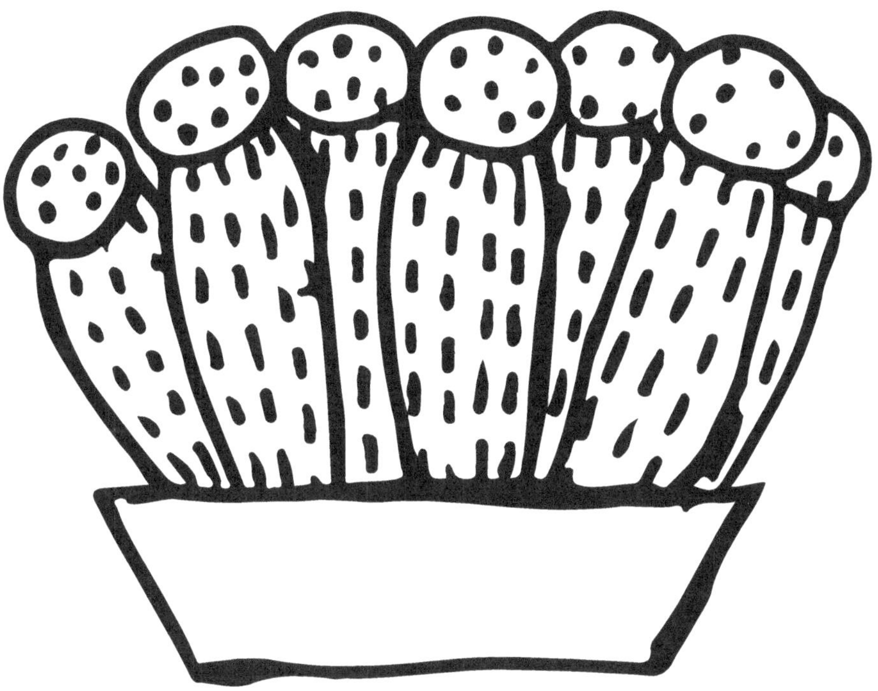

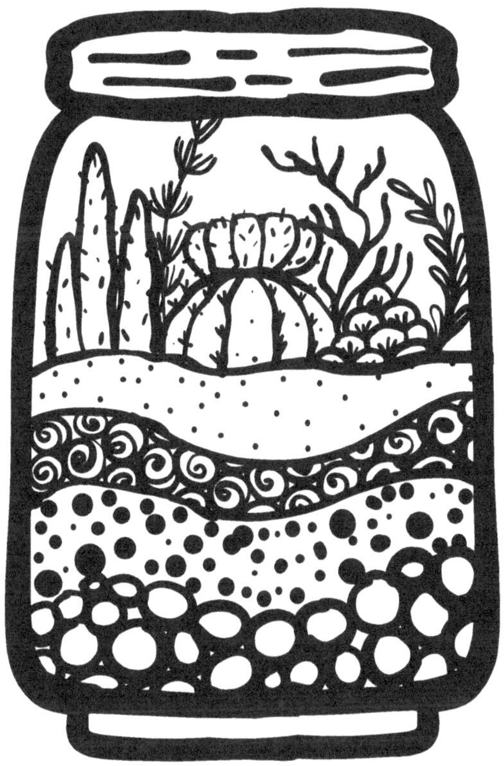

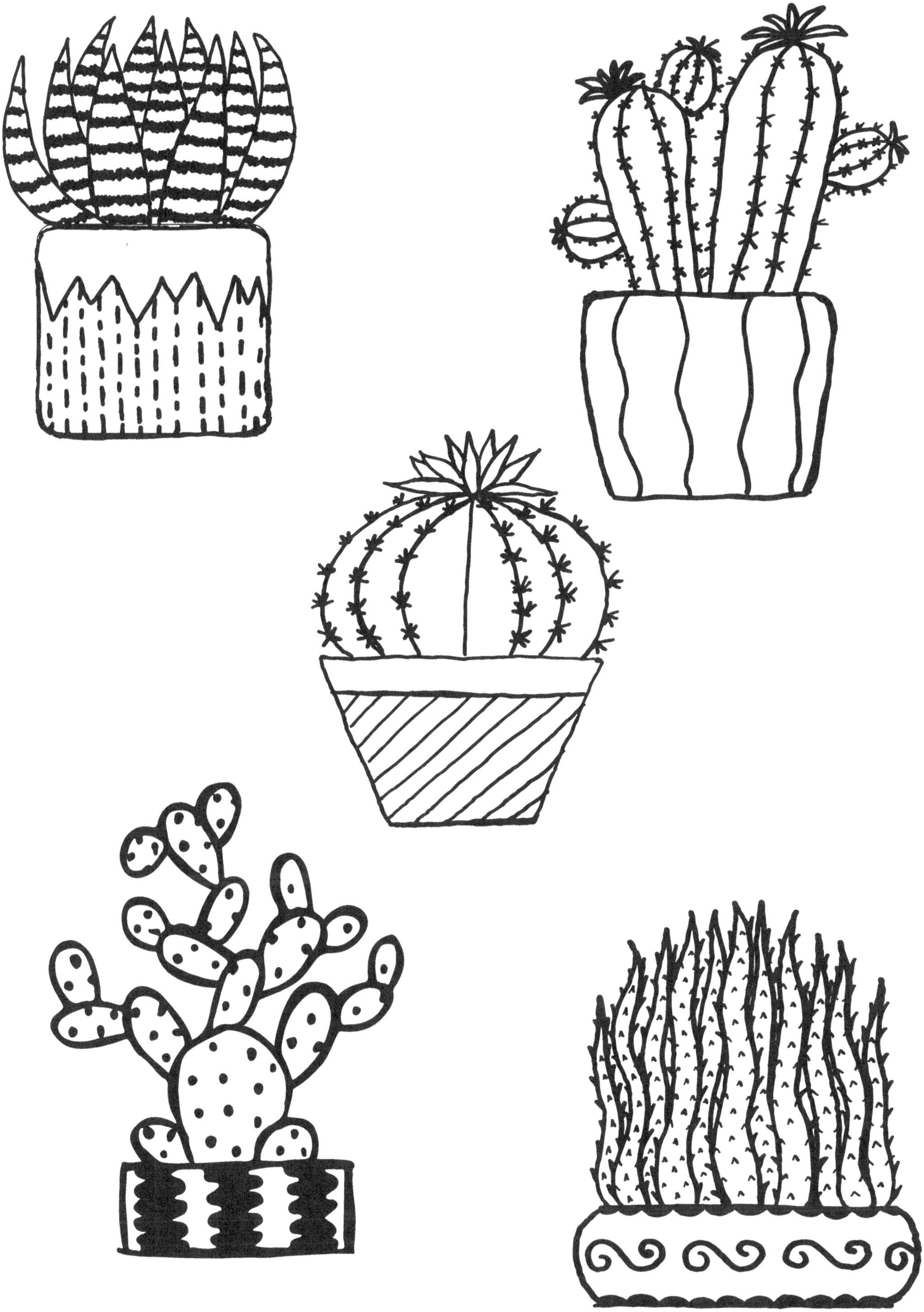

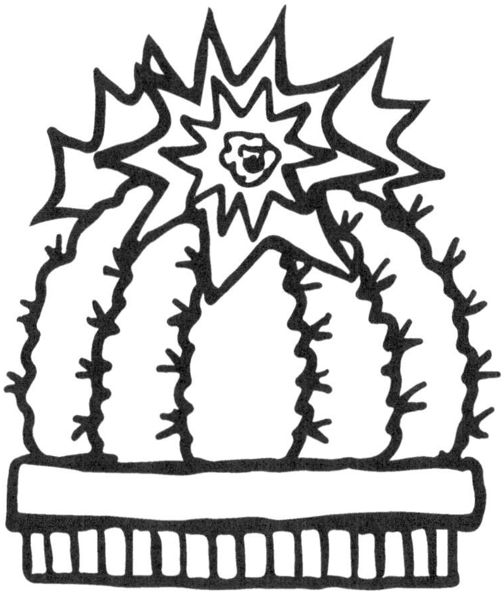
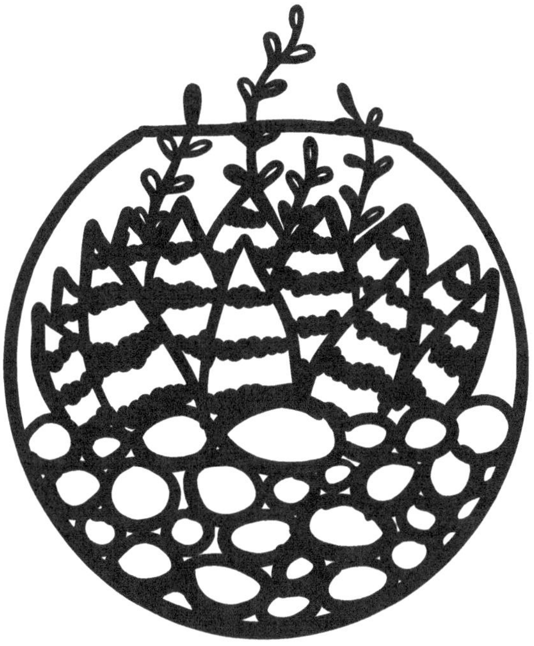
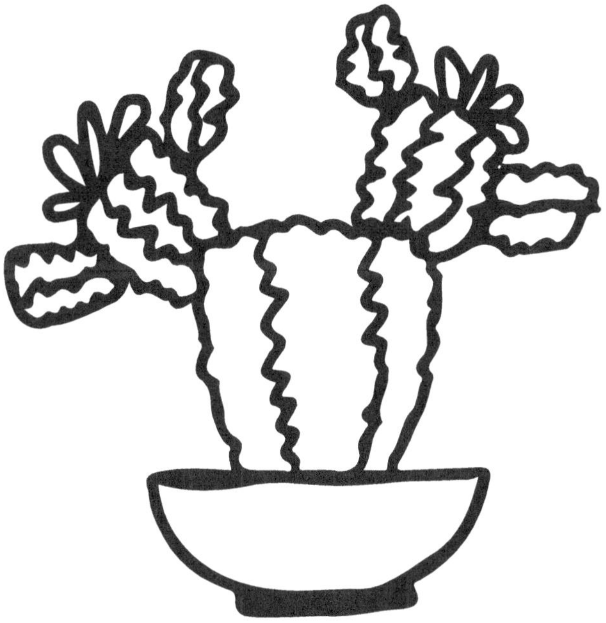
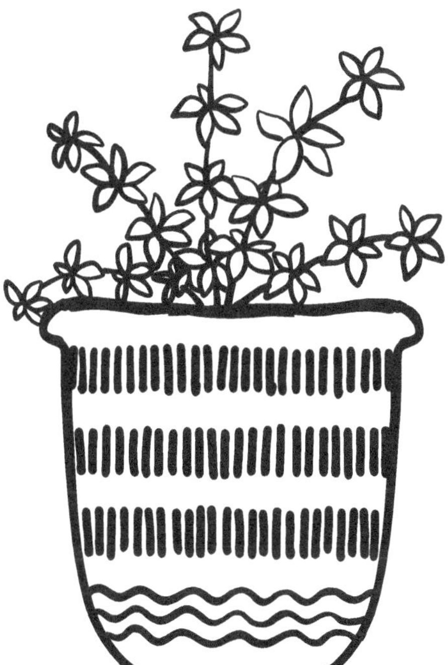

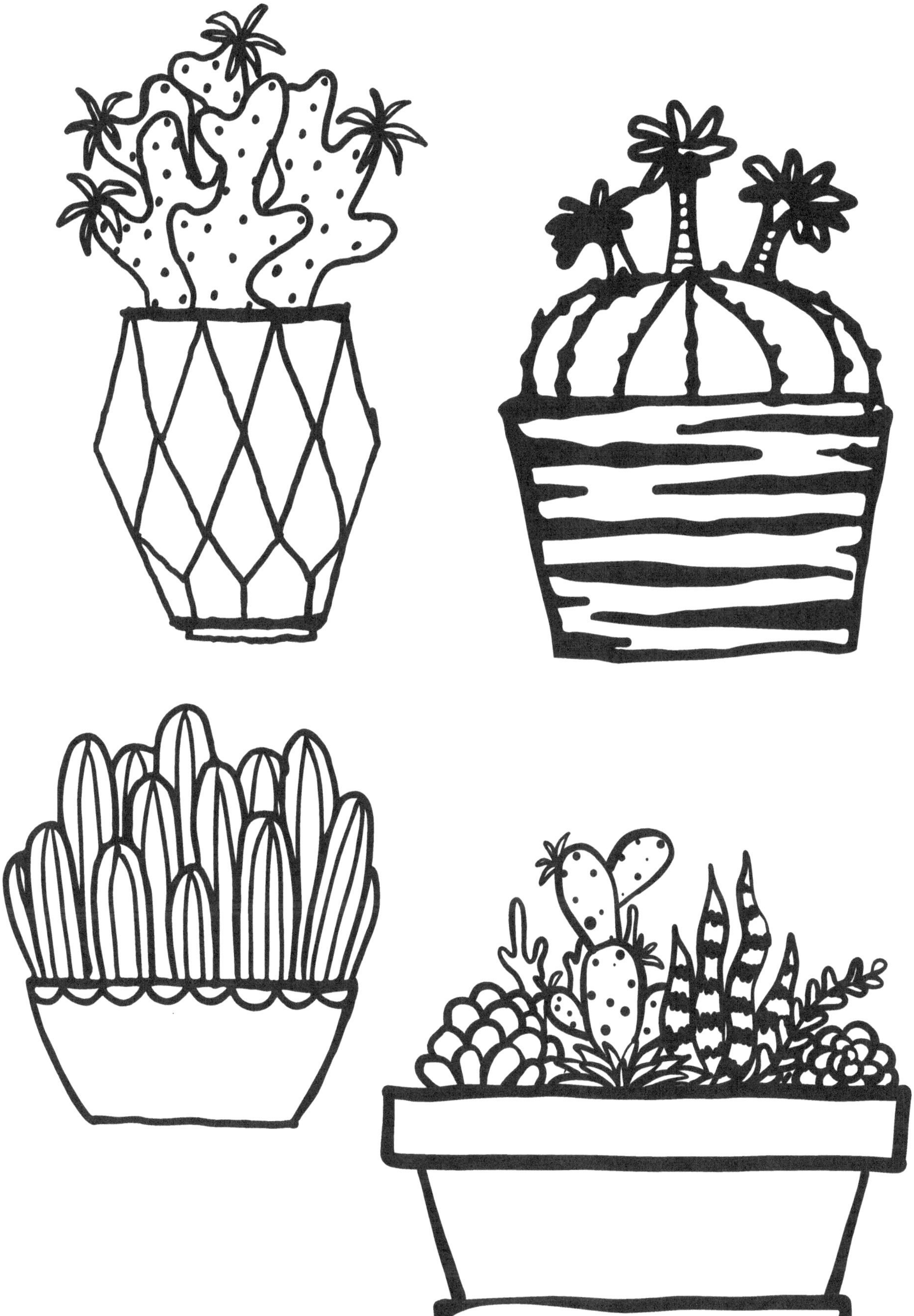

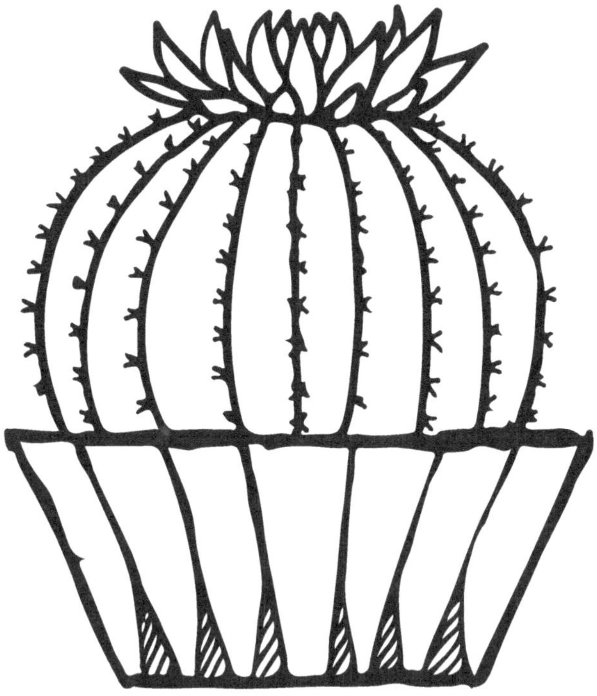
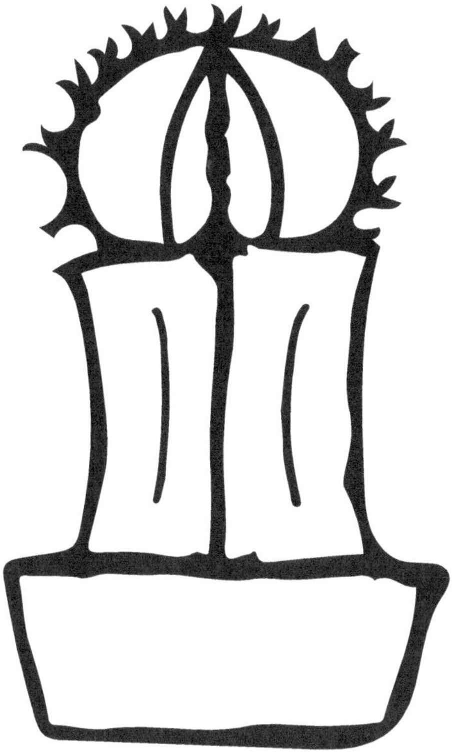
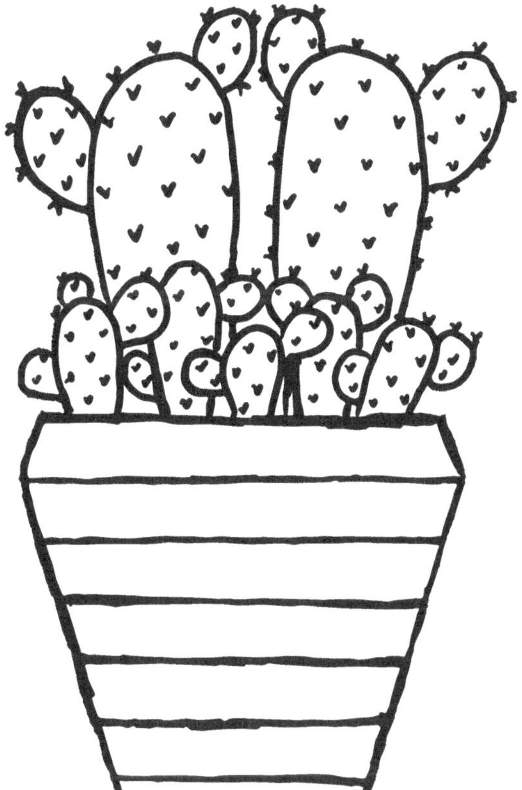
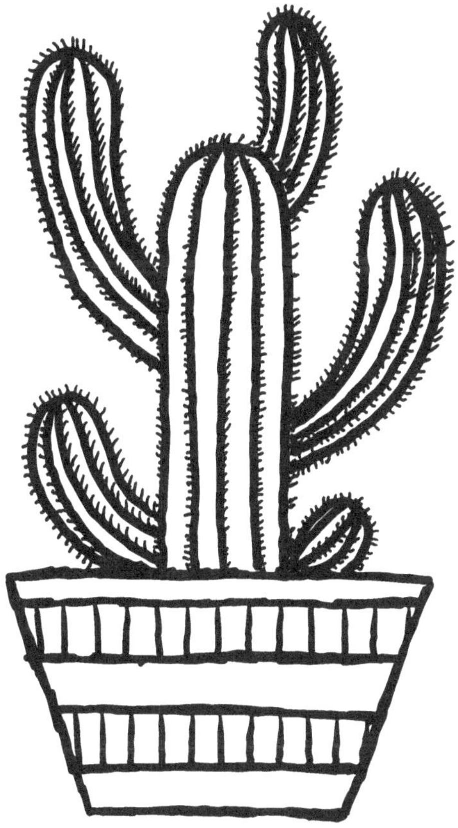

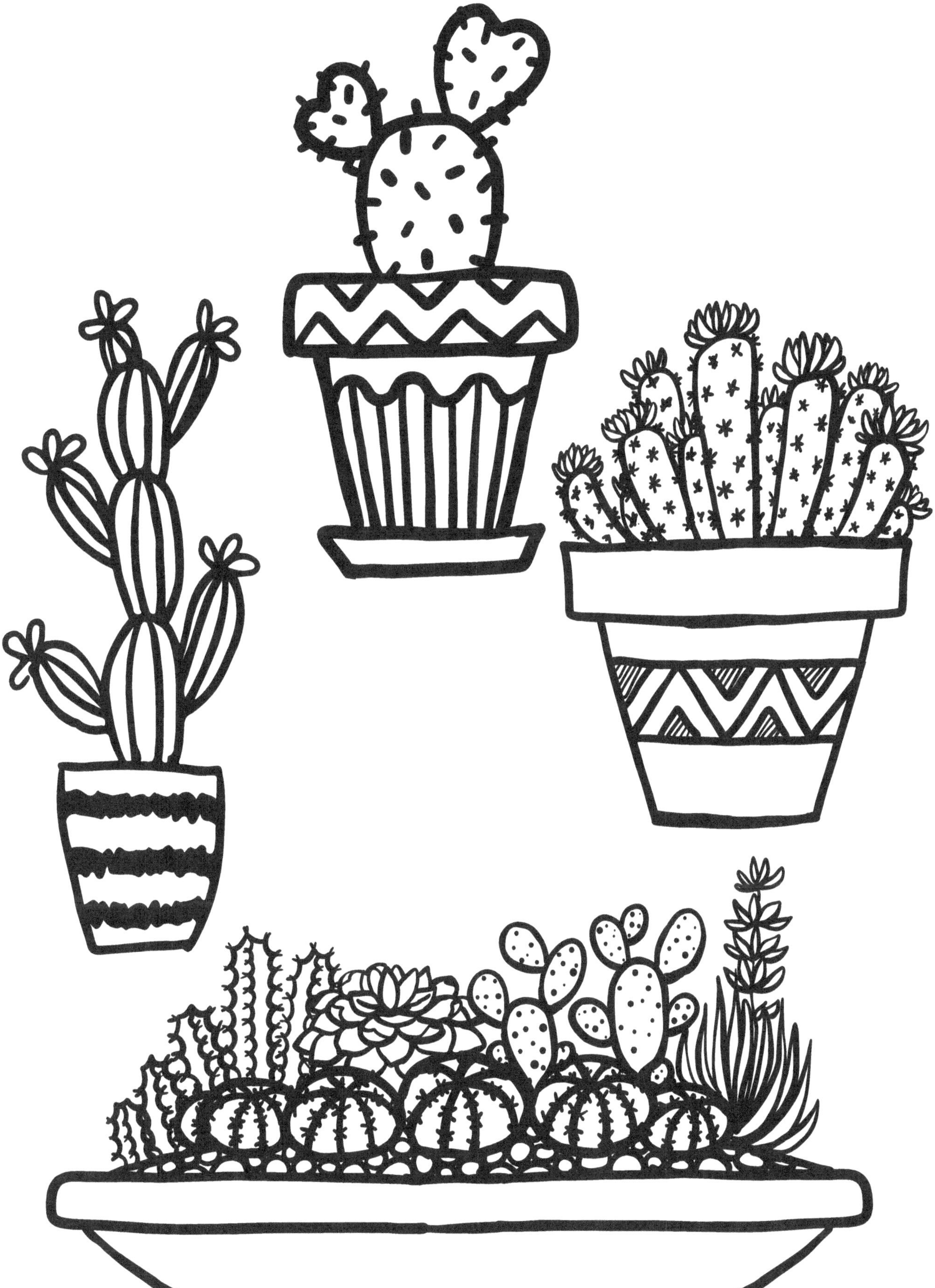

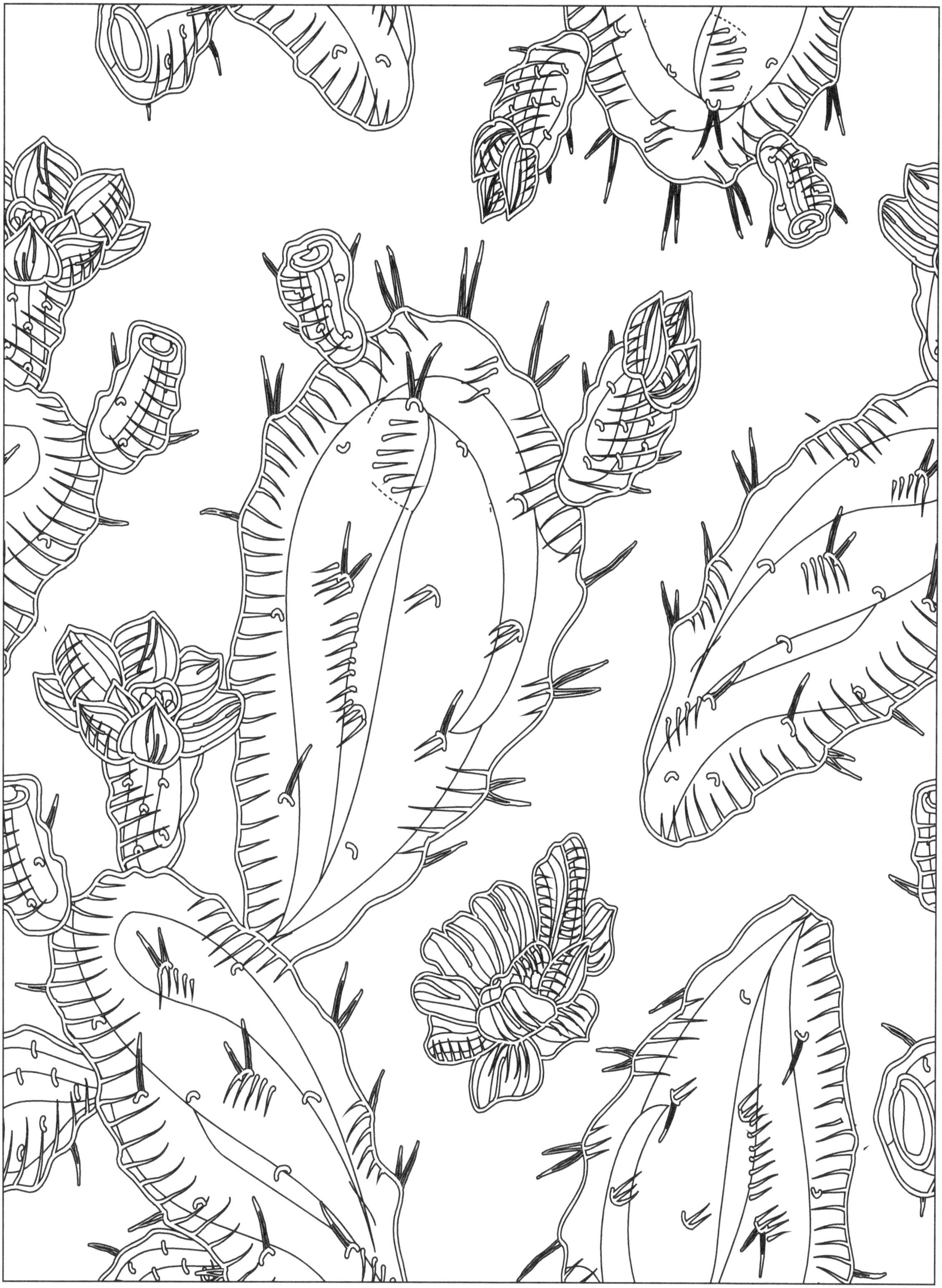

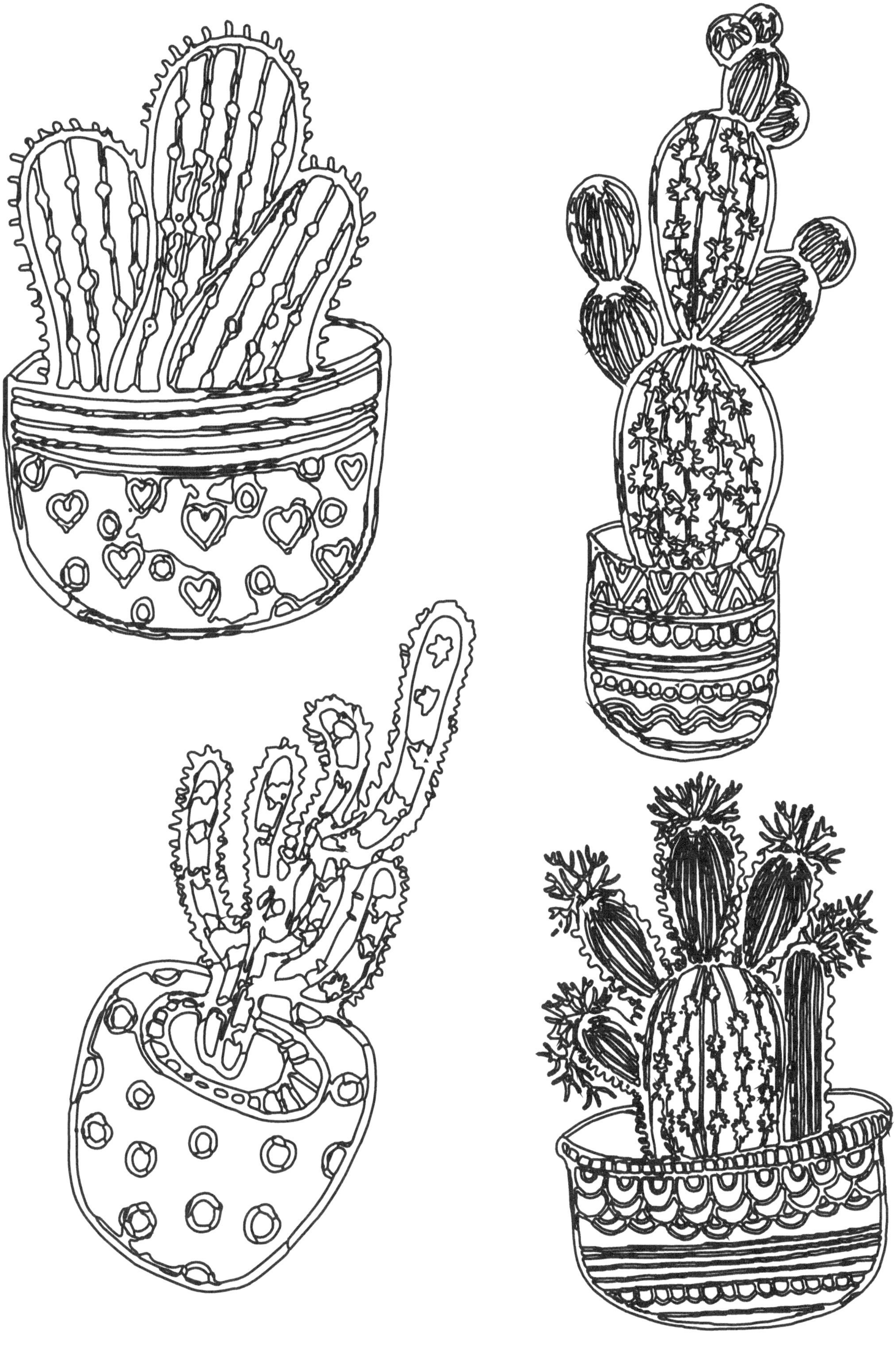

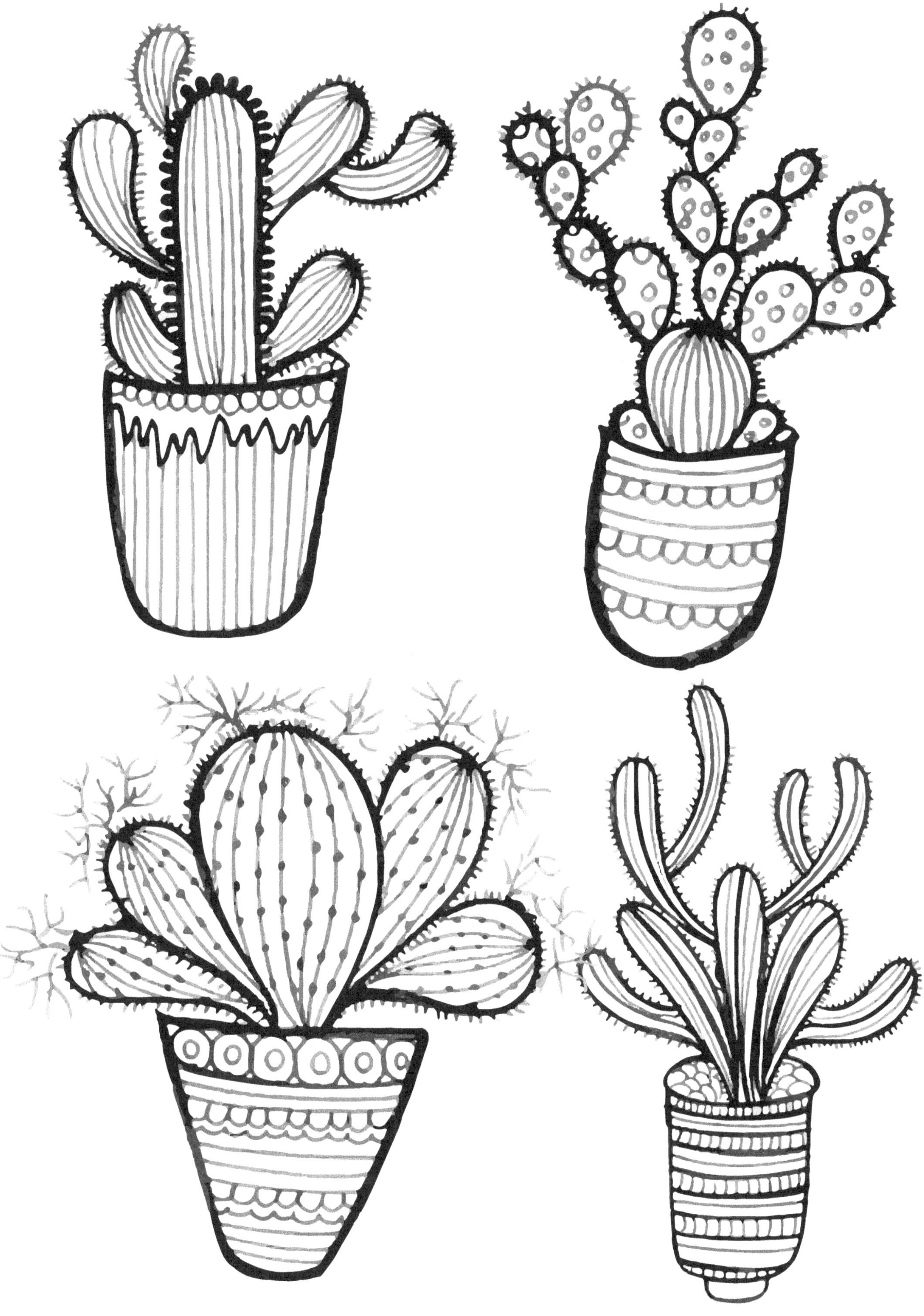

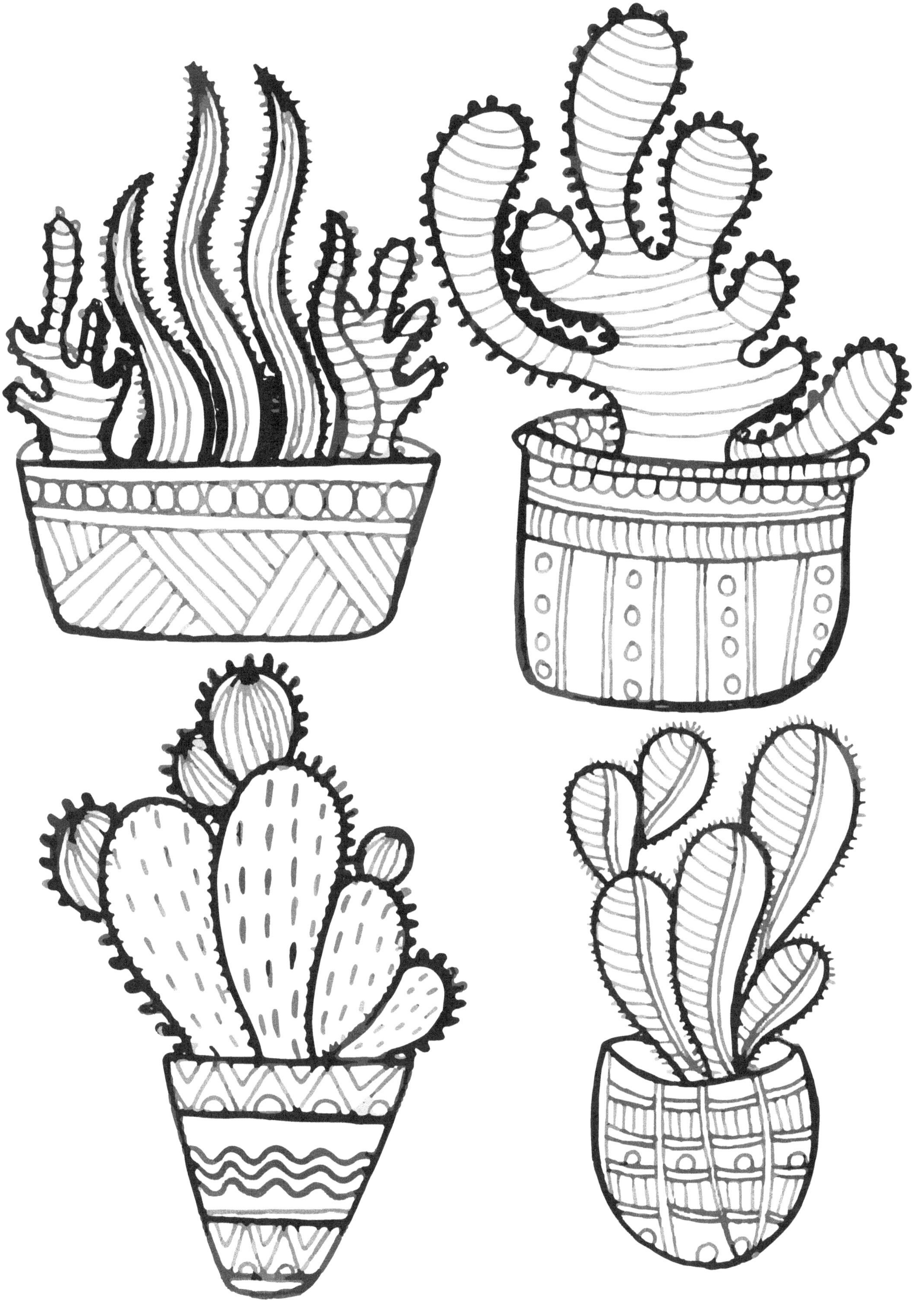

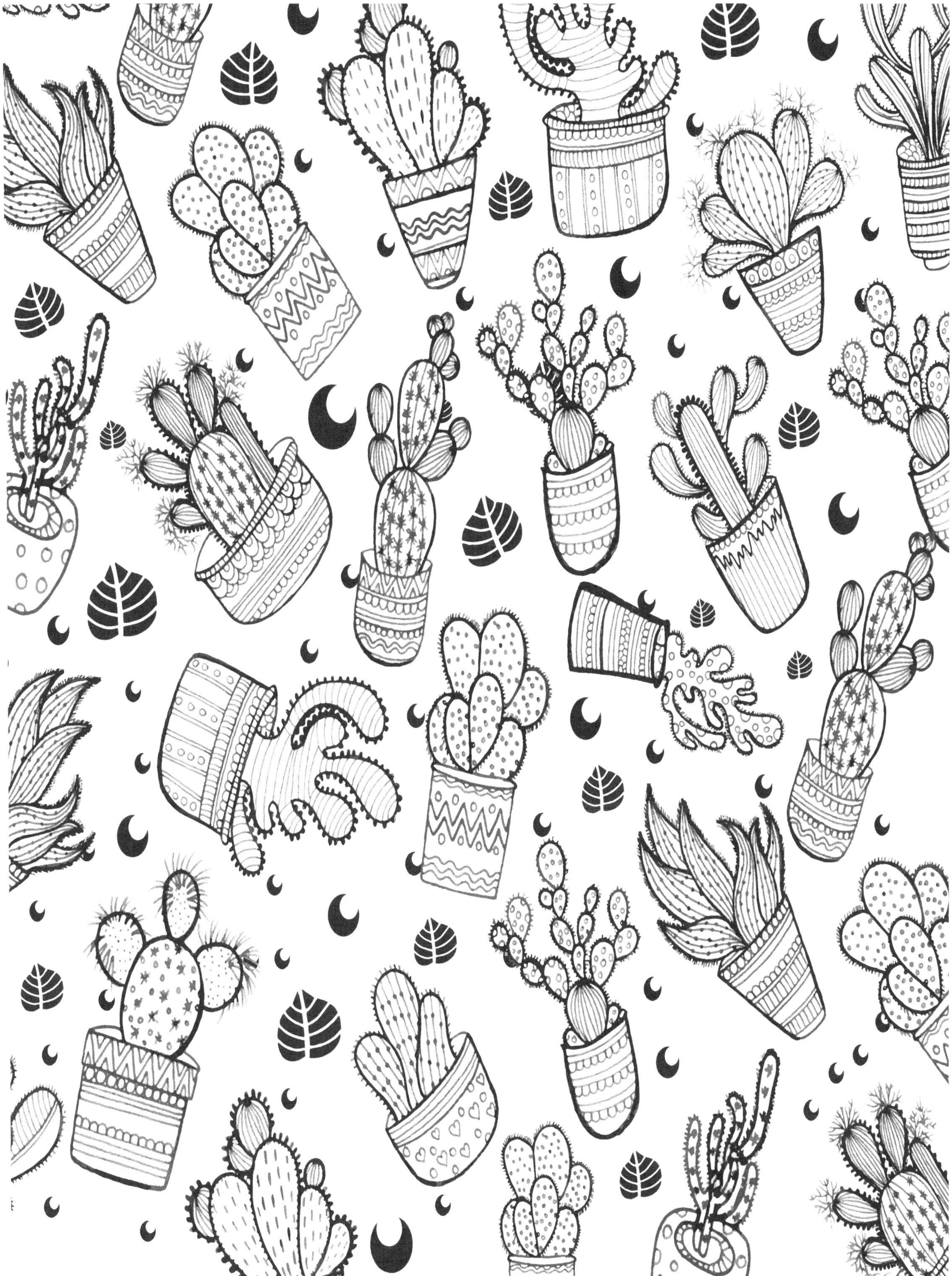

www.ingramcontent.com/pod-product-compliance
Lightning Source LLC
Chambersburg PA
CBHW082354220526
45470CB00008B/2741